QUIET MOMENTS

of

Faith

for

MOMS

QUIET MOMENTS
of
Faith
for
MOMS

Ellen Banks Elwell

CROSSWAY BOOKS • WHEATON, ILLINOIS
A DIVISION OF GOOD NEWS PUBLISHERS

Quiet Moments of Faith for Moms

Copyright © 1999 by Ellen Banks Elwell

Published by Crossway Books
    A division of Good News Publishers
    1300 Crescent Street
    Wheaton, Illinois 60187

Cover and Interior designed by: Design Point Inc.

First printing, 1999

Printed in the United States of America

Library of Congress Cataloging-in-Publication Data

Elwell, Ellen Banks, 1952-
  Quiet moments of faith for moms / Ellen Banks Elwell.
    p. cm.
  Includes bibliographical references.
  ISBN 1-58134-129-6 (hardcover : alk. paper)
  1. Mothers Prayer-books and devotions—English. 2. Devotional
 calendars. I. Title.
 BV4847.E57 1999
 242'.6431—dc21   99-35237
                     CIP

15	14	13	12	11	10	09	08	07	06	05	04	03	02	01	00	99
15	14	13	12	11	10	9	8	7	6	5	4	3	2	1		

To

Kathy,

My cousin and friend

Contents

Introduction

The story is told of a man attempting to cross the frozen St. Lawrence River in Canada. Unsure of whether the ice would hold, the man first tested it by laying one hand on it. Then he got down on his knees and gingerly began making his way across the ice. When he got to the middle of the frozen river, where he trembled with fear, he heard a noise behind him. Looking back, he saw a team of horses pulling a carriage down the road toward the river. Upon reaching the river, the horses didn't stop but bolted right onto the ice and drove past him while he sat there on all fours.

Sometimes our journey of faith is like that. We come up against an obstacle or a frightening experience, and we feel uncertain about how to proceed or where to place our confidence. Perhaps our faith seems weak or even nonexistent. At times like these, it's good for us to be reminded of the faith-journeys of other people—some who lived in Bible times and some who live now.

Quiet Moments of Faith for Moms includes five devotional readings per week, all related to a weekly topic, with suggested Bible readings for weekends or extra days. Some readings address the mother-child relationship directly, while others focus on the growth of our souls as women.

Each daily reading begins with a Bible verse or verses and ends with a short prayer, encouraging us to extend our thanks, needs, confessions, and praise to God, who loves us immeasurably and wants us to spend time with Him.

My hope is that in this book you will find truth, encouragement, direction, and hope. May it be a frame for your own faith, pointing always to Christ, who is the author and finisher of our faith.

Ellen Banks Elwell, 1999

1

Faith

PART ONE

ONE
Faith

*Our children too shall serve him, for they shall hear from us about
the wonders of the Lord; generations yet unborn shall hear
of all the miracles He did for us.*

PSALM 22:30-31, TLB

I like to read out loud to my sons—sometimes I even read
to my seventeen-year-old early on weekday mornings to
wake him up. (This process wakes him up gradually and
then he isn't so grumpy!) A little later in the morning I read
to my eleven-year-old (we're currently reading *Black
Beauty*). In the evenings I read to them from the Bible.
Several months ago when I was reading the story of Moses
to my youngest son, Jordan, he commented, "I'm sure glad
I didn't have to grow up with a substitute mother!"

As you recall, the king of Egypt had instructed the
Hebrew midwives to kill all of the Hebrew baby boys.
Being a woman of faith, Moses' mother, Jochebed, put him
in a basket and hid him among the reeds of a river. His
older sister Miriam kept an eye on the basket until
Pharaoh's daughter found him. In God's plan, Miriam
asked the princess if she should find a nurse for the child,

and so Moses' very own mother was able to raise him for some years before he was educated in Pharaoh's palace.

Can you imagine how often Jochebed must have retold that story to Moses and Miriam and Aaron before Moses went to live in the palace? The siblings grew up hearing that God sees and God provides. Later in their lives God used them to lead His people out of Egypt. When God provides for us, we can encourage our children's faith by telling them what God has done for us.

God who sees and provides,
Thank You for providing us with children to nurture and love. Please help us to notice Your provisions and then to rehearse them with our children, strengthening our faith and encouraging theirs. Amen.

TWO

Faith

*hen he said to Thomas, "Put your finger here; see my hands.
Reach out your hand and put it into my side.
Stop doubting and believe."*

JOHN 20:27

Although Thomas was one of Jesus' disciples, he had great difficulty believing Jesus had really risen from the dead. Hence the name "Doubting Thomas."

After Jesus' resurrection, Thomas was not present when Jesus first appeared to His disciples. When Thomas heard of Jesus' appearance, he said he wouldn't believe it unless he felt Jesus' hands and side. Eight days later they met, and Jesus invited Thomas to touch His wounds. Thomas' beautiful response—"My Lord and My God!"—prompted St. Augustine to say that Thomas doubted so that we might believe.

The struggle of Thomas to believe offers us hope. If Jesus showed patience and willingness to help Thomas believe, He will do the same for us. Jesus spoke of even greater blessing for the heart of the person who believes *without* seeing.

When there is no star on the bosom of night, and no friendly voice in the solitude, to believe then is to get very near the heart of him who on the cross clung to the Father in the midnight darkness.[1]

These words from F. B. Meyer prompt me to remember the words of a favorite hymn, "Near to the Heart of God":

> *There is a place of quiet rest near to the heart of God,*
> *A place where sin cannot molest, near to the heart of God.*
> *O Jesus, blest Redeemer, sent from the heart of God,*
> *Hold us who wait before Thee near to the heart of God.*[2]

Father,
We confess our lack of faith. Thank You that Thomas's experience helps us to believe in You. Amen.

THREE
Faith

Therefore, since we have been justified through faith, we have peace with God through our Lord Jesus Christ.

ROMANS 5:1

In the middle of the night in a small Midwest farming community, the two-story house of a young family caught fire. Quickly everyone made their way through the smoke-filled house out into the front yard. Everyone except a five-year-old boy. The father looked up to the boy's room and saw his son crying at the window, rubbing his eyes.

The father knew better than to re-enter the house to rescue his son, so he yelled, "Son, jump! I'll catch you." Between sobs, the boy responded to the voice he knew so well. "But I can't see you."

The father answered with great assurance. "No, son, you can't, but I can see you!" The boy jumped and was safe in his father's arms.[3]

The commitment this young boy made reminds me of the commitment we make when we decide to put our trust in Jesus. In the boy's helplessness, his father came to save him. In our helplessness, God came to save us. He didn't come to us because of our strength — He came to us because of our *weakness*. As a result of Jesus' death and our faith, Romans 5:1-5 tells us, we receive peace with God, access to God, hope, confidence amidst the daily trials of life, and a personal experience with God's love. If we realize that He died for us to save us from our sin, we see our helplessness and realize that jumping into His arms is a very wise choice. In fact, it's the only way we can live!

Father,
Thank You that You always see us, no matter where we are. Thank You that in our helplessness You sent Jesus to save us. Amen.

FOUR

Faith

*Fight the good fight of the faith. Take hold of the eternal life
to which you were called when you made your good confession
in the presence of many witnesses.*
1 TIMOTHY 6:12

> Doubt is natural within faith. It comes because of our
> human weakness and frailty. . . . Unbelief is the decision
> to live your life as if there were no God. It is a deliberate
> decision to reject Jesus Christ and all that He stands for.
> But doubt is something quite different. Doubt arises
> within the context of faith. It is a wistful longing to be sure
> of the things in which we trust. But it is not and need not
> be a problem.
>
> ALISTER MCGRATH[4]

Faith is not easy. To fight for faith is to strive vigorously
for it, but also to struggle *against* our adversary, the devil.
First Timothy 6:12 is set in the context of a chapter that
commands us to do three things—flee, follow, and fight.
We are to flee from pride, the love of money, and false
teachings; follow after righteousness, godliness, faith, love,

endurance and gentleness; and fight *for* faith and *against* the world, the flesh, and the devil.

For a mom who is depressed, for a mom whose husband is involved in addictive behavior, for a mom whose child is hanging out with unwholesome friends, there are plenty of doubts and struggles—she's clearly in a fight. As we fight against the world, the flesh, and the devil through the power of God's Word and Spirit, we "take hold of the eternal life"—we grab it, setting our hope not on fleeting things but on God who gives eternal life and is Himself hope.

Father,
Please give us strength as we fight the good fight of faith. Thank You that You have promised You will always be with us. Please help us to grab hold of Your promises when doubts rise in our minds and hearts. Amen.

FIVE
Faith

So then, just as you received Christ Jesus as Lord, continue to live in him, rooted and built up in him, strengthened in the faith as you were taught, and overflowing with thankfulness. See to it that no one takes you captive through hollow and deceptive philosophy, which depends on human tradition and the basic principles of this world rather than on Christ.

COLOSSIANS 2:6-8

When I was in my preteens, my father gave me the assignment of cutting sixty-four two-by-fours to a certain length. To assist me, he cut one board and told me he wanted them all the size of that pattern. I used that pattern to cut the first board. Then I picked up the board I had cut and marked the next board and used that board to mark the next and continued on in this manner until I was through. It wasn't until I completed the project that I saw my error; the last board was several inches longer than the pattern I was given. I was reminded that the pattern of faith that I need for the foundation to my life must be primary, not two or three generations away. I must go directly to the source.[5]

As Christian moms, we desire to see our children grow in their faith in Christ. Just as our Christian life begins and grows through *our* faith in Christ, so theirs must begin and grow because of *their* faith in Christ. We can encourage this by nurturing our children's hearts through time in God's Word.

If our children are not rooted in Christ and grounded in God's Word, they can be drawn into a belief system that isn't true, resulting in behavior that is not wholesome. We want our children to believe not only that Christ is important but that He is everything!

Father,
Please help me to point my child to personal faith in Christ through time spent in Your Word. Amen.

EXTRA READINGS FOR DAYS 6 AND 7
James 1:1-12; Hebrews 11:1-40

2

Faith

PART TWO

ONE

Faith

Consider it pure joy, my brothers, whenever you face trials of many kinds, because you know that the testing of your faith develops perseverance. Perseverance must finish its work so that you may be mature and complete, not lacking anything. *(italics mine)*
JAMES 1:2-4

During my college days at Moody Bible Institute, I was a resident assistant in the women's dormitory, overseeing life on the sixth floor of Houghton Hall. Returning to my room late one evening, I opened the door with my key, stepped in, and was convinced that I had the wrong room—it was completely empty. After rechecking and realizing that I had the right room, I noticed that the room wasn't *completely* empty. There was a Bible passage on the wall—James 1:2-4 (quoted above).

Well, it was pretty hard not to smile at my situation in light of the last three words of the verse! The ladies of sixth floor had moved everything out of the room, storing half of the furniture in the shower room and the other half on the roof! (They kindly helped me move it back.)

When the serious trials of life come and we choose to

cry out to God for His strength and wisdom, we experience significant growth in Christian character. At a point in my life when I was going through a very tough experience, a friend suggested that I begin a Faith Affirmations Notebook. On days that I struggled for faith and hope, it was extremely helpful to document the many, many ways God had shown His love and care for me. I know difficult experiences have produced growth in character because they remind me of how much God cares for me, and how much I need Him.

God,
Trials are so hard, and they often are accompanied with gut-wrenching
pain to our souls or bodies. At times when we feel like giving up, please
give us faith to persevere. Amen.

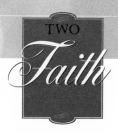

TWO

Faith

He [Jesus] also said, "This is what the kingdom of God is like. A man scatters seed on the ground. Night and day, whether he sleeps or gets up, the seed sprouts and grows, though he does not know how."
MARK 4:26-27

For any mom who likes to garden, here's an object lesson to try with your kids. During the fall, take your child to a garden store and purchase bulbs for tulips or daffodils. The children can see pictures on the packages showing them what colors their flowers will be.

After you make a plan for which bulbs go where, plant them with your children. If they haven't planted bulbs before, the kids will be amazed to learn that in five or six months the bulbs will begin to shoot up from the ground, grow, and finally bloom. The activity of planting bulbs will probably raise some questions. Why don't we wait until the warm weather to plant them? Why do we have to wait so long for them to come up? How do we know they will really be red?

The questions children have about planting bulbs are similar to some of the questions we have about our

Christian faith. In both situations we learn that we need to follow the instructions and wait for God to work. When we plant bulbs, we trust the instructions on the package, wait for growth, and then enjoy the beauty. The same is true of our faith. We trust the instructions God has given us in the Bible, we choose to obey His guidelines and direction for our lives, and then we wait for the beauty! We also learn that growth doesn't happen immediately—it takes time.

God,
Thank You for Your Word, which gives us instructions on how to plant seeds of faith and godliness. Please give us patience as we trust You for growth. Amen.

Be self-controlled and alert. Your enemy the devil prowls around like a roaring lion looking for someone to devour. Resist him, standing firm in the faith, because you know that your brothers throughout the world are undergoing the same kind of sufferings.

1 PETER 5:8-9

The Bible teaches us that Satan is our adversary—a liar and a murderer. He slanders, accuses, and deceives, and his lies are his chief weapons. In order for us to recognize and counteract his deceptions, we must *know* and *believe* God's truth. We don't resist by running away from the enemy; we resist by standing up to him with the Word of God— through *faith*.

When Jesus was tempted by the devil in Matthew 4, He responded to the devil's three temptations with Scripture, not with His divine power. That is encouraging to us because we too can respond with Scripture. When Satan tempted Jesus with hunger, a desire of the flesh, Jesus responded with Deuteronomy 8:3: "Man does not live on bread alone but on every word that comes from the mouth of the LORD." If I cater to my physical needs and ignore God's will for me, I sin.

Satan's second temptation involved misquoting Scripture and daring Jesus to intervene by rescuing Himself, and Jesus responded with Deuteronomy 6:16, saying it is wrong to tempt God. It is wrong to put ourselves in circumstances where we try to force God to do something on our behalf.

The third time around, Satan offered Jesus a shortcut in exchange for worship, but Jesus responded with Deuteronomy 6:13, which says that whatever we worship is what we serve. If Jesus, who is the Son of God, chose to resist the devil with faith in God and surrender to His Word, how much more do *we* need to!

Father,
When we meet up with the devil's lies, please help us to recognize them and counteract them with Your truth. Thank You for Your Word. May we hide it in our hearts so that we will not sin. Amen.

FOUR

Faith

When Jesus looked up and saw a great crowd coming toward him,
he said to Philip, "Where shall we buy bread for these people to eat?"
He asked this only to test him, for he already had in mind
what he was going to do.
JOHN 6:5-6

Jesus was sitting on a hill with his disciples when He looked up and saw a large crowd coming. "Where shall we buy bread for these people to eat?" He asked Philip. Jesus asked Philip this question to "test" him, because Jesus already knew there was no obvious human solution to this problem.

Philip responded with a bigger problem. He was trying to think logically, and he realized that it would take eight months' wages just to give each person one bite of food!

As he did with Philip, Jesus sometimes tests us by putting us in difficult situations with no easy answers. At these times we feel frustrated, as Philip did. However, frustration cannot be God's intended result. The wise disciple always keeps the door open for God to work. When the first or second look at a problem yields no solution, do you trust in God to work or assume it's hopeless? Philip fell short because he allowed his thinking to be limited by his own limited resources instead of seeking God's limitless resources.[6]

Andrew spoke up and presented Jesus with two things—a lunch and another problem. A young boy had a lunch of five rolls and two fish; the problem was, the boy's lunch wasn't enough to feed everyone. But Jesus demonstrated that the little boy's lunch, offered in faith, was *more than enough*. Before the boy witnessed a great work of God, he had to make a sacrifice and step out in faith. Are we willing to do the same?

God of all provisions,
Thank You that You had such patience with Your disciples, and thank You that You show patience to us. May we remember that You have limitless resources, and may we be willing to trust You. Amen.

FIVE

Faith

Therefore, since we are surrounded by such a great cloud of witnesses, let us throw off everything that hinders and the sin that so easily entangles, and let us run with perseverance the race marked out for us. Let us fix our eyes on Jesus, the author and perfecter of our faith, who for the joy set before him endured the cross, scorning its shame, and sat down at the right hand of the throne of God.

HEBREWS 12:1-2

Peter Cameron Scott was born in Glasgow in 1867 and became founder of the Africa Inland Mission. But his beginnings in Africa were anything but auspicious. His first trip to Africa ended in a severe attack of malaria that sent him home. He resolved to return after recuperation.

This return was especially gratifying to Scott, because this time his brother John joined him. But before long John was struck down by fever. All alone, Peter buried his brother, and in the agony of those days recommitted himself to preaching the gospel in Africa. Yet again his health gave way and he had to return to England.

How would he ever pull out of the desolation and depression of those days? He had pledged himself to God. But where could he find the strength to go back again to Africa? With man it was impossible!

He found the strength in Westminster Abbey. David Livingston's tomb is there. Scott entered quietly, found the tomb, and knelt in front of it to pray. The inscription reads,

OTHER SHEEP I HAVE WHICH ARE NOT OF THIS FOLD; THEM I ALSO MUST BRING. (John 10:16)

He arose from his knees with a new hope. He returned to Africa. And the mission he founded is a vibrant, growing force for the gospel today in Africa.[7]

A mom of faith is one who focuses on God and the increase of His kingdom amid all the hustle and bustle of each day's activities. Does that mean she never gets discouraged? No way! But she prays for the encouragement she needs to keep going.

Father,
Some days we get so weary and discouraged that it's difficult to keep going. May we focus on You and run to You for help and encouragement. Thanks that You care and listen. Amen.

EXTRA READINGS FOR DAYS 6 AND 7
Ephesians 2:8-9; John 20:24-31

3

The Bible

ONE

The Bible

*But as for you, continue in what you have learned and have become
convinced of, because you know those from whom you learned it, and
how from infancy you have known the holy Scriptures, which are able
to make you wise for salvation through faith in Christ Jesus.
All Scripture is God-breathed and is useful for teaching, rebuking,
correcting and training in righteousness, so that the man of God
may be thoroughly equipped for every good work.*
2 TIMOTHY 3:14-17

I am grateful to have grown up in a home where the Word
of God was honored and taught. My parents, Sunday
school teachers, and youth leaders all treated the Bible with
great respect; and as a result, my love for God's Word has
grown through the years.

The New Testament character Timothy, a friend of the
apostle Paul, was the son of a Gentile father and a Jewish-
Christian mother. In spite of the fact that Timothy's father
was probably not a believer, Timothy received a great
heritage from his mother and grandmother, being taught
the Scriptures from a very young age. His mother and
grandmother not only taught him the truth—they guided

him into spiritual understanding. The truth led him to belief that ultimately led to salvation in Christ. Truth—faith—salvation—the pattern of Timothy's family is a pattern for us all.

God's Word brought Timothy to salvation, but it also provided everything he needed for effective Christian living—doctrine, reproof, correction, and instruction.

> In the stern experiences of life there is no stay that is comparable to the Holy Scriptures. The infinite variety of Scripture adapts itself to different states of the soul. Whatever our need, we can find its solace and remedy here. Thus, we may live a complete life, finding in the Bible resources for all our emergencies.[8]

The Bible helps transform a new Christian into a mature person in Christ. The longer we live the Christian life, the more we realize our need for God's Word.

Father,
Thank You for Your Word. Thank You for the example of Timothy's mother and grandmother, who taught him to love and obey Your Word. Please give us wisdom and grace with our children as we try to do the same. Amen.

TWO

The Bible

Your word is a lamp to my feet and a light for my path.
PSALM 119:105

Joanne Shetler, a missionary to the Balangao tribe in the northern part of the Philippines, was on a helicopter flight to deliver cement, glass, and nails for the tribe's new hospital clinic. As the helicopter descended, something went terribly wrong, and the helicopter crashed. At first Joanne feared she might be burned to death, but after the Balangaos dug and yanked to get her out, she squirmed loose of the wreckage. Blood from gashes on her head mixed and hardened with the cement powder that covered her body, burning her eyes and filling her lungs. That long night was torturous.

While Joanne waited for help throughout the night, the Balangao people worked their way through the throng, touched her hand, and prayed, "God, don't let her die — the Book's not done yet. Please let her live; the Book's not done yet." You see, Joanne was translating the Bible into the Balangaos' language, so they could hear the words of the God who speaks. Because they were hungry to hear more of God's Word, they prayed for the life of the missionary who had been sent to them.

Joannne recovered from the accident and finished the translation of the Bible into the Balangao language, and many lives were brought from darkness to light. When Joanne's work there was done and she was ready to board a plane home, Ama, a Balangao man, sent her home with this blessing: "Thank you. Thank you. Thank you for coming. I never would have known about God if you hadn't come."[9]

God who loves the whole world,
Thank You that Your Word lights our path. May we read and study Your Word carefully, hiding it in our hearts so we can share it with others who also need to hear Your words. Amen.

THREE

The Bible

God's laws are perfect. They protect us, make us wise, and give us joy and light. God's laws are pure, eternal, just. They are more desirable than gold. They are sweeter than honey dripping from a honeycomb. For they warn us away from harm and give success to those who obey them.
PSALM 19:7-11, TLB

Warning our children away from harm and pointing them toward success is what we want for them, right? We teach them not to touch the burner on the stove because we don't want them to be burned. We instruct them not to play in the street because we don't want them to get hit by a car. We teach them to do their homework and study for tests so they can enjoy the success of learning. We give them physical laws to follow because we want the best for them.

Since we moms care deeply about our children, it shouldn't surprise us that God gave us laws for our spiritual well-being. But I'm amazed at how many parents present their kids with "ideas" as opposed to laws.

In a recent survey of 3,000 couples conducted by *Bride's* magazine, only 4 percent of the women and 1 percent of the men reported that they were virgins when they married. That was depressing news, as was a newspaper article written by a parent who said that abstinence before marriage is a fine idea, but that it is only an opinion.

What would happen if I taught my child that not exceeding the speed limit is only an opinion? God didn't give ten opinions on Mt. Sinai—He gave the Ten Commandments, all of which point to Christ, who is the ultimate fulfillment of all God's requirements.

Just as we physically protect our children, God has graciously established laws for our *spiritual* protection. His laws are based on truth and goodness—a sign of His great love and care.

Father,
Thank You that as we obey Your Word, we experience protection, wisdom, joy, and light. Amen.

FOUR

The Bible

ll men are like grass, and all their glory is like the flowers of the field. The grass withers and the flowers fall, because the breath of the LORD blows on them. Surely the people are grass. The grass withers and the flowers fall, but the word of our God stands forever."

ISAIAH 40:6-8

I have always loved reading these verses from Isaiah because of the last phrase, "but the word of our God stands forever." Those few words remind me that God's Word has an *eternal* shelf life. Unlike grass or flowers, it never dies. Throughout the Bible we are likened to grass, as a reminder of our human frailty. Lest we get to thinking we are invincible and will live here forever, God's Word points out that our earthly lives are temporary.

In Palestine, grass is green from April through October, when there's plenty of rain. But when the dry season comes, the grass dries up and withers. Flowers provide us with another example of the transience of our lives. Flowers are beautiful and wonderful! They bud, sprout, and burst forth with color and aroma. When flowers from our gardens hit that bursting point, we sometimes cut them, bringing them into our houses to enjoy in a vase or an arrangement. But whether we leave them growing outside or bring them inside, individual flowers and blooms last only a short time.

When we contrast the length of bloom our lives have with the length of bloom the Scriptures have, we realize that we can never put too much emphasis on God's Word. In all the demands of motherhood, it's so easy for us to let other seemingly urgent things crowd out our reading, meditating upon, and praying over God's Word, but in the context of eternity, what is most lasting and important?

God of the Bible,
Thank You for the incredible value and life of Your Word. May I make time each day to read it, and then may I choose to obey it.

FIVE

The Bible

*As the rain and snow come down from heaven and stay upon
the ground to water the earth, and cause the grain to grow and
to produce seed for the farmer and bread for the hungry, so also
is my Word. I send it out and it always produces fruit.
It shall accomplish all I want it to, and prosper everywhere I send it.*

ISAIAH 55:10-11, TLB

The rain and snow that falls from clouds to give the world
fresh supplies of water keeps living things growing and
existing. In the central areas of South America, which
receive over sixty inches of rainfall a year, life forms flourish.
But in places like Northern Africa, where there is less than
ten inches of rainfall a year, the land is dry and treeless.

I love the verses from Isaiah that liken rain and snow to
God's Word. I especially appreciate the progression of the
action: the precipitation comes down, stays, waters, causes
grain to grow, produces seed, and makes bread. That's
what rain and snow do for people, and that's what God's
Word does for us.

It *comes down* — possibly during a church service, or
while a mother reads a Bible story at bedtime, or through a
neighborhood Bible study.

It *stays*. Just as moisture is absorbed into the ground, God's Word is absorbed into our hearts.

It *waters*. Revelation 22:17 says, "Whoever is thirsty, let him come; and whoever wishes, let him take the free gift of the water of life."

It *causes grain to grow*. When God's Word sprouts in our hearts, it's like the grain—first the stalk appears, then the head, and then the full kernel, producing more seed. Growth takes time!

It *produces seed*. The new seed dies, takes root, sprouts, and grows as it is nurtured. God's Word is necessary for all of these stages of growth.

It *produces bread*; it *gives life*. The Word of God leads us to an eternal relationship with Jesus, who is the bread of life (John 6:35).

Father,
Thank You for the rain and snow You provide to water the earth.
Thank You for Your Word, which points us to a growing relationship
with Jesus, the bread of life. May we be faithful in guiding our children
to Your Word. Amen.

EXTRA READINGS FOR DAYS 6 AND 7
Psalm 119:9-16; Psalm 119:89-96

4

Redemption

ONE

Redemption

*In him we have redemption through his blood, the forgiveness of sins,
in accordance with the riches of God's grace that he lavished
on us with all wisdom and understanding.*

EPHESIANS 1:7-8

During their elementary years, my sons rode bikes to school when weather permitted. One day Nate walked home, forgetting that he'd ridden his bike. Around dinnertime he remembered, but when he went back to get the bike, it was gone. First, we felt sad with him about his loss, and later we discussed the importance of locks and bike registration.

When Nate became the happy owner of a replacement bike, my husband and I made sure he used a bike lock, and we also decided to register the bike at the police station. On the Saturday that my husband took Nate to the police station to register, a police auction was taking place. You can imagine their surprise when one of the items to be auctioned off was the bike that Nate had left at school! My husband spoke with the officer in charge, who told him that if he could come up with some proof of ownership,

Nate could have the bike back. Jim and Nate zipped home, picked up some papers, and later returned with the lost bike!

That evening at dinner we used the story of the bike to explain the meaning of redemption to our children. To redeem is to recover ownership or to rescue. When Jesus died on the cross, He provided redemption to rescue us from sin. Our family's redemption of the bike was very satisfying, but it was not costly. When Jesus redeemed us, it cost Him His life's blood. That's how much He loves us!

Great Redeemer,
We are amazed at how much You love us. On days when we lack hope and faith, help us to remember Your amazing gift of love. Amen.

TWO

Redemption

I *will free you from being slaves to them and I will redeem you with an outstretched arm and with mighty acts of judgment."*
EXODUS 6:6

The Hebrew people had been slaves in Egypt for 400 years when God spoke to Moses from a burning bush, calling him to lead the Hebrew people out of Egypt. Three elements of redemption, all present in the deliverance of the Israelites from Egypt, are (1) freedom from bondage, (2) the payment of a redemption price, and (3) an intermediary who secures the redemption.

In the Exodus the children of Israel were given freedom from slavery and taskmasters. The price of redemption was the blood of a lamb sprinkled on the door frame of each home. And God was clearly the Redeemer, bringing His people out of Egypt with His outstretched arm and mighty acts of judgment.

This Old Testament story of redemption painted a picture of a much bigger and better redemption that was yet to come—a redemption that would provide freedom for *us*.

The lamb that was killed in every Israeli home that night was in some ways like our Savior. The lamb died for the people, and its blood saved them. That is what happened again many years later, when Christ the Savior came as the Lamb of God to die for each of us.

And just as God passed over those who had the marks of the lamb's blood on their houses, and did not punish them, so it will be when Christ comes back again. He will not punish those who have the mark of the Savior's blood in their hearts—those whose hearts have been cleansed from sin by his blood.[10]

Father,
Thank You for the picture of the blood of lambs sprinkled on doors that helps us explain redemption to our children. May we always remember that our freedom from sin is possible only because we trust in the blood of Jesus, our Redeemer. Amen.

THREE
Redemption

At one time we too were foolish, disobedient, deceived and enslaved by all kinds of passions and pleasures. We lived in malice and envy, being hated and hating one another. But when the kindness and love of God our Savior appeared, he saved us, not because of righteous things we had done, but because of his mercy. He saved us through the washing of rebirth and renewal by the Holy Spirit, whom he poured out on us generously through Jesus Christ our Savior, so that having been justified by his grace, we might become heirs having the hope of eternal life.

TITUS 3:3-7

When I was a child, my parents used to collect S & H Green Stamps. The stamps were given for purchases made at various stores, and when a whole book of stamps was filled, it could be redeemed at an S & H Green Stamp center for a gift of the customer's choice. The formula for redemption was: Purchase + Stamps = gift.

God's redemption is surprisingly different. Instead of offering our purchases to God, the things we offer are our foolishness, disobedience, deceit, enslavement, malice, envy, and hatred. Ugh! And what is God's part? What does He bring to the equation? He shows us kindness and love.

Jesus Christ chose to die for us not because of anything good we had done, but because of His mercy. When we believe, He gives us the washing of rebirth and the renewal of the Holy Spirit, treats us as though we hadn't sinned, and calls us God's children!

It was the astounding realization of this equation that prompted John Newton to pen the words to the song "Amazing Grace." He was a seaman from a young age who became captain of his own slave ship, capturing, selling, and transporting black slaves to plantations in America and the West Indies. On one of Newton's voyages he came across Thomas á Kempis's book *Imitation of Christ*, saw his debauchery, and came to Christ.

As a result he began crusading *against* slavery and became an Anglican pastor. What an amazing change God's redemption brings to our lives!

A Prayer of Praise
"Amazing grace—how sweet the sound—
That saved a wretch like me!
I once was lost but now am found,
Was blind but now I see."

FOUR
Redemption

For you know that it was not with perishable things such as silver or gold that you were redeemed from the empty way of life handed down to you from your forefathers, but with the precious blood of Christ, a lamb without blemish or defect.

1 PETER 1:18-19

How much does redemption cost? For Loung Ung, the price for her redemption was her mother's jewelry.

Loung experienced a very traumatic childhood in Cambodia under the rule of the Khmer Rouge. Because her father had been a government official in a previous regime, the Khmer Rouge took him to prison. Hoping to protect the children, Loung's mother sent them all off to different orphanages, but shortly before Vietnam invaded Cambodia, Loung's parents and some of her siblings died. Loung managed to reconnect with her brother in a refugee camp, and six months later they sold their mother's jewelry for passage to Vietnam, hiding in a boat underneath a pile of dead fish.

Loung eventually came to the United States, later graduated from college, and worked for a while with battered women. But several years ago she took a trip back to Cambodia. After sitting through a memorial service that included the names of thirty of her relatives killed during the reign of terror, she decided to dedicate her life to Cambodian causes. She said, "My whole life is just about being redeemed."

Having experienced incredible trauma at the hands of a corrupt government, Loung was moved to serve because she knew what she had been redeemed from. Our redemption as believers was not paid for with jewelry — it cost Jesus His blood. When we realize what Jesus did for us and all the rottenness he has saved us from, we become motivated to serve Him with grateful hearts. Like Loung, we can say, "My whole life is just about being redeemed."

Great Redeemer,
Thank You that You were willing to redeem us by paying for our sins with Your blood. May we serve You with grateful hearts. Amen.

FIVE

Redemption

Preach the Word; be prepared in season and out of season; correct, rebuke and encourage — with great patience and careful instruction.
2 TIMOTHY 4:2

Does someone in your circle of family or friends need redemption? Someone you care about who needs deliverance from sin? When Jesus met up with the Samaritan woman at the well (John 4), He knew that was *exactly* what she needed. She was living in sin, having been married five times and at that time living with a man who wasn't even her husband. It's interesting to observe how Jesus dealt with her. He knew that before she could experience saving faith, she needed to be convicted of her sin.

> The only way to prepare the soil of the heart for the seed is to plow it up with conviction. That was why Jesus told her to go get her husband: He forced her to admit her sin. There can be no conversion without conviction. There must first be conviction and repentance, and then there can be saving faith. Jesus had aroused her mind and stirred her emotions, but He also had to touch her conscience, and that meant dealing with her sin.[11]

Since I am not God, I cannot see into other people's hearts, convict them of their sin, or change them. But there are some things I can do. I can share God's Word, and I can pray. When I do, I am joining hands with God in preparing another person's soul for the good news of God's redemption!

Father,
I pray for _____. According to the truth of John 16:8, please convict her or him of guilt in regard to sin, righteousness, and judgment. Amen.

EXTRA READINGS FOR DAYS 6 AND 7
Ephesians 1; 1 Peter 1:3-9

5

Thanks

ONE
Thanks

Because of the LORD's great love we are not consumed,
for his compassions never fail. They are new every morning;
great is your faithfulness.

LAMENTATIONS 3:22-23

If one should give me a dish of sand and tell me there were particles of iron in it, I might look for them with my eyes and search for them with my clumsy fingers and be unable to detect them; but let me take a magnet and sweep through it and now would it draw to itself the most invisible particles by the mere power of attraction. The unthankful heart, like my finger in the sand, discovers no mercies; but let the thankful heart sweep through the day and as the magnet finds the iron, so it will find, in every hour, some heavenly blessings, only the iron in God's sand is gold!

HENRY WARD BEECHER[12]

There are a lot of things that I do *daily*. I walk, shower, read my Bible, feed the cat, bring in the mail, and read the newspaper. There are a lot of things God does daily too, and I decided to try jotting some of them down one day to prompt my thankfulness. It wasn't hard. He brought the sun up this morning. He sustained the crickets that I heard chirping. He provided the pleasant breeze I enjoyed while I was out walking. He oversaw the growth of the juicy peach I had for lunch. He brought the sun down. He gave me strength to meet the needs of the day.

A thankful heart prompts a good attitude. Because God's blessings are new every morning, it's good for us to keep our thanks current for what He supplies *each day*.

God our provider,
May we choose daily to have a grateful heart because You are faithful.
Amen.

TWO

Thanks

S̄ave us, O L̄ord our God, and gather us from the nations, that we may give thanks to your holy name and glory in your praise.
PSALM 106:47

Have you ever noticed that a grateful person is not usually a miserable person? I'm not suggesting that a grateful person never gets sick, never gets angry, never loses a job, or never encounters challenges in relationships. But a grateful person has an attractive manner. Psalm 106 encourages us to be thankful for the goodness of the Lord and also gives us some pictures of what life was like for the Israelites when they *weren't* thankful. Their path toward misery included:

- Giving no thought to God's miracles.
- Not remembering the kindness of the Lord.
- Rebelling.
- Not waiting for God's counsel.
- Giving in to their cravings.
- Growing envious.
- Worshiping false idols.
- Not believing God's promises.

- Grumbling in their tents.
- Provoking God by their wicked deeds.
- Mingling with the nations and adopting their customs.
- Defiling themselves morally.

In spite of the fact that the Israelites' lack of thankfulness to God led them into all kinds of sin, when they cried to God out of their distress, He heard them and helped them. God's patience and mercy in dealing with them was truly astounding. There is so much we can learn from the Israelites. We easily fall into the same patterns of grumbling, complaining, and forgetting the God who has saved and blessed us. May we remember that God inhabits the hearts of people who thank and praise Him, but people who grumble and rebel lead miserable lives. It's our choice.

Father,
May we choose to look for things to thank You for every day, rehearsing the blessings You have given us. Amen.

THREE

Thanks

*or the LORD is good and his love endures forever; his faithfulness
continues through all generations.*
PSALM 100:5

Do you have certain people or things in your life that
remind you of how much you have to be thankful for?
When I see my youngest son running around, I'm reminded
how thankful I am that the femur bone in his left leg
mended after a skateboard accident. Whenever I see or
hear from our young friend Drew, I'm thankful that God
healed his body after a three-year bout with leukemia.

I practiced my violin today and thanked God for
providing it. About a year before I turned forty, I began
praying about the possibility of purchasing a new violin,
since I was still playing the same student violin I'd had back
in junior high school. I only prayed about it occasionally,
probably because I didn't think of a new violin as a
necessity.

Without my parents knowing what I was praying, they
had been thinking about buying me a new violin for my
fortieth birthday. Imagine my shock when they called me

several months before my birthday and suggested that I begin shopping around for violins because they wanted to give me one for my birthday! I remember my knees getting all jelly-like when they told me. Not only was I grateful for the generosity of my parents, but I was amazed that God would provide a new violin in a method I wouldn't ever have imagined.

As I practice my violin this week for the prelude and offertory at church on Sunday, I offer thanks for the creative ways God answers our prayers!

God,
Thank You that You see and provide. Thanks for specific events in our lives that strengthen our faith in You. Amen.

FOUR

Thanks

It is good to say, "Thank you" to the Lord, to sing praises to the God who is above all gods. Every morning tell him, "Thank you for your kindness," and every evening rejoice in all his faithfulness.

PSALM 92:1-2, TLB

Four forms of thanks in prayer that we can use and model for our children are:

1. *Give thanks for provisions.* Psalm 75:1, TLB says, "How we thank you, Lord! Your mighty miracles give proof that you care." We can thank God for food, breath, strength, light, encouragement, protection, and any other provisions each day.

2. *Give thanks in all situations.* First Thessalonians 5:18 urges us to "Give thanks in all circumstances, for this is God's will for you in Christ Jesus." One of my friends reminded me that the verse doesn't say give thanks *for* all things but *in* all things. We don't say thanks for the problem, but we thank God for what He's accomplishing in us through the problem.

3. *Give thanks for what God is doing in people's lives.* In 1 Thessalonians 1:2-3 Paul states, "We always thank God for

all of you, mentioning you in our prayers. We continually remember before our God and Father your work produced by faith, your labor prompted by love, and your endurance inspired by hope in our Lord Jesus Christ." These are very specific areas of growth—"work produced by faith," "labor prompted by love," and "endurance inspired by hope."

4. *Give thanks in anticipation of what God will yet do*. Philippians 4:6 says, "Do not be anxious about anything, but in everything, by prayer and petition, with thanksgiving, present your requests to God." God desires thanks, which indicates our trust in Him.

Offer thanks for provisions, in all circumstances, for God's work in our lives and in anticipation of what He *will* do!

Father,
Thanks for Your Word. Thanks for hope to keep going. Thanks that You are in control even when we feel off-balance. Thanks that You will be with us throughout the day. Amen.

FIVE

Thanks

All this is for your benefit, so that the grace that is reaching more and more people may cause thanksgiving to overflow to the glory of God.
2 CORINTHIANS 4:15

Have the words "Thank you" ever prompted you to cry? Last week I had blocked out the two weeks before a writing deadline to do nothing but write and compile. That was before my oldest son, Chad, called. He said that two of his college friends, Scott and Erin, were coming to Wheaton for a few days before Erin left on a missions trip to Africa, and would I be able to help with a little hospitality and housing? Due to putting clean sheets on beds, cleaning bathrooms, and doing some baking in preparation for my guests, I lost a little bit of work time, but the note I found on a pillow after Scott left this morning more than made up for it.

> Mrs. Elwell, Thanks so much for letting me stay here last night. It was nice having somewhere to feel welcome after our long drive yesterday. We both appreciate your hospitality, especially as Erin is a little nervous about her trip. We had a good time chatting last night. God has

already blessed Erin's trip through you. Thanks again. —
Scott and Erin

That's when I cried! I realized that in God's schedule,
being an encouragement to them was an important
interlude in the middle of my work, and I was actually
energized by the encouragement of their thanks. When we
thank other people, it offers more encouragement than we
will ever know.

Father,
Thank You for the encouragement You send us through the gratefulness
of other believers. May we be quick to offer thanks to others and quick
to offer thanks to You! Amen.

EXTRA READINGS FOR DAYS 6 AND 7
Psalm 107; Psalm 100

6

Worship

ONE

Worship

"Now I, Nebuchadnezzar, praise and exalt and glorify the King of heaven, because everything he does is right and all his ways are just. And those who walk in pride he is able to humble."

DANIEL 4:37

Worship happens only when we're humble; true worship never happens when we're proud. Nebuchadnezzar learned the hard way that nothing in our lives is more insane than human pride. But there is also nothing more sensible and sober than praising God. Having made an arrogant boast about all his achievements, Nebuchad-nezzar was stricken down at the height of his pride by God's judgment and literally lived in insanity for a while. But when he raised his eyes to heaven and praised God, his sanity was restored. We sometimes forget one of the benefits of worship: when we lift our eyes to heaven, our perspective changes.

Nebuchadnezzar left us a wonderful pattern for worship:

• We lift our eyes, which means taking them off our present circumstances.

- We see ourselves as nothing in comparison with Him who is everything, prompting us to realize how much He loves us.
- We see that God is much bigger than ourselves—He is eternal.
- We thank Him that His faithfulness is passed from generation to generation.
- We realize that it is not ours to say to God, "What have You done?" because all power in heaven and earth is His.

The life of Nebuchadnezzar displays to us that true worship doesn't happen when we're pretending to be someone we're not or when we feel self-righteous and deny our need for God's mercy and grace. True worship begins with humility and even helps restore our sanity!

Father,
Thank You for Your wonder and Your splendor. Thank You that You are everything and that You love and care for us. May we worship You as You deserve to be worshiped. Amen.

TWO

Worship

After they had heard the king, they went on their way, and the star they had seen in the east went ahead of them until it stopped over the place where the child was. When they saw the star, they were overjoyed. On coming to the house, they saw the child with his mother Mary, and they bowed down and worshiped him. Then they opened their treasures and presented him with gifts of gold and of incense and of myrrh. And having been warned in a dream not to go back to Herod, they returned to their country by another route.

MATTHEW 2:9-12

The wise men were probably astrologers who, in their eagerness to observe the stars in the heavens, encountered a sign from God. In an amazing way God broke into the world of the wise men by showing them the star in the east and later redirecting their trip to thwart the murderous plans of Herod and his advisers. What was the reaction of the wise men to all this? They worshiped, they opened their treasures, and they presented gifts to Jesus. When we realize that God has broken into our world, we learn that He desires the same reaction from us. He wants us to bow down in adoration of all He is and all He has done, open our hearts to Him, and present Him with our lives.

As with gladness men of old did the guiding star behold—
As with joy they hailed its light, leading onward, beaming bright—
So, most gracious Lord, may we evermore be led to Thee.
As with joyful steps they sped to that lowly manger bed,
There to bend the knee before Him whom heav'n and earth adore,
So may we with willing feet ever seek the mercy seat.
As they offered gifts most rare at that manger rude and bare,
So may we with holy joy, pure and free from sin's alloy,
All our costliest treasures bring, Christ, to Thee, our heavenly King.
Holy Jesus, ev'ry day keep us in the narrow way;
And, when earthly things are past, bring our ransomed souls at last
Where they need no star to guide, where no clouds Thy glory hide.[13]

Father,
Help us worship, follow, and obey You day by day, and may we help
others, especially our children, do likewise.

THREE

Worship

When the LORD made a covenant with the Israelites, he commanded them: "Do not worship any other gods or bow down to them, serve them or sacrifice to them. But the LORD, who brought you up out of Egypt with mighty power and outstretched arm, is the one you must worship. To him you shall bow down and to him offer sacrifices."
2 KINGS 17:35-36

In these verses we see that God does not wish to have worship of Him shared with anyone or anything else. After 250 years of rebellion and sin, the nation of Israel was taken captive by Assyria. The Assyrians had a policy of taking the best citizens to their own land and then colonizing the captive land with foreigners they had taken from other countries. This is how the Samaritan people came about—they were a mixed breed.

At first there was no religious faith in Samaria, so the leaders approached the problem in an unusual way. They imported a Jewish priest to instruct the people about the Lord, but then they had the people worship both Jehovah and the national gods. But God didn't want mixed worship. All through the Bible he asks for undivided hearts. Many times in the Old Testament God had stretched out His arm to reach His people where they were and save them from their troubles, and yet they didn't get it. He was the only one they were supposed to worship!

> Too many people feel that they ought to do something to show their respect for God. They attend to the outward forms of worship, lest they should lose status; but in their hearts they enthrone worldly and worthless ideals.[14]

Sometimes we think that without renouncing other gods, we can give God some sort of obligatory recognition. But He wants our undivided attention and praise.

Father,
Thank You for Your mighty, outstretched arm that throughout the ages has reached people where they were and saved them from distress. Forgive us for running to other things—other gods. May we serve You with undivided hearts. Amen.

Worship

*Therefore, I urge you, brothers, in view of God's mercy,
to offer your bodies as living sacrifices, holy and pleasing to
God—which is your spiritual worship.*

ROMANS 12:1

In the Old Testament, worship of God involved altars, the tabernacle, lampstands, burnt offerings, priestly garments, priests, anointing oil, and incense. But in the New Testament, worship is characterized by joy and thanksgiving for the redemption Christ graciously provided for us through His death on the cross. The New Testament instructs us that *where* we worship God is not so important as *how* we worship. Worship includes prayer, praise, and God's Word, and it must be done in spirit and in truth.

When our minds and bodies are yielded to God, every day can be a worship experience. Psalm 96:9, TLB, says, "Worship the Lord with the beauty of holy lives." But worshiping God requires freedom from slavery or service to anything else, and if we are selfishly holding on to things in our lives that are contrary to God's instructions for us, our attempts at worship are not only jokes—they are actually mockery of God.

What prompts us to present ourselves to God? Not laws, shoulds, or ought-tos. A view of God's mercy is what motivates our true worship. It's been said that grace is getting what we don't deserve and mercy is not getting what we do deserve. As we daily thank God for His mercy to us and remember all He's done for us, we are prompted to worship Him with the beauty of holy lives.

Father,
"When all thy mercies, O my God, My rising soul surveys, Transported with the view, I'm lost in wonder, love, and praise."[15]

FIVE

Worship

*He then brought me into the inner court of the house of the LORD,
and there at the entrance to the temple, between the portico
and the altar, were about twenty-five men. With their backs toward
the temple of the LORD and their faces toward the east,
they were bowing down to the sun in the east.*

EZEKIEL 8:16

Ezekiel was a priest who, along with other citizens of Judah, lived as a captive in Babylonia. During this period of time he was a powerful messenger of God, pointing out that each person's individual response to God determines his or her eternal destiny.

More specifically, it's who or what we worship that determines our spiritual destiny. In the verses above, Ezekiel observed priests who were worshiping the sun. Admittedly, the sun is awesome. It gives us light, it rises and sets each day, it gives off heat, and it is a stable and predictable point of reference seen by human beings everywhere. But the sun is not God. Rather, the sun points *to* God.

We run into trouble when we worship the things God

has made instead of worshiping Him. Taking a trip to Brookfield Zoo in Chicago is a worshipful experience for me. To think that God imagined and created the giraffe with its long neck, the zebra with its stripes, and the polar bear who loves to play in the water helps me remember how big God is!

God deserves our worship throughout each day. Going to the grocery store with our child and acknowledging the great variety of fruits and vegetables that God created is worship. Watching a cat give birth to kittens can lead to worship. The question is, in all the exciting, awesome things of life, do we give credit to God, or do we consistently worship the things?

Father,
Forgive us for paying more attention to things You have made than to You. May our hearts be inspired to give You worship each day for what You have created and provided. Amen.

EXTRA READINGS FOR DAYS 6 AND 7
Daniel 4:19-37; Matthew 2:1-12

7

What Christians Believe

PART ONE

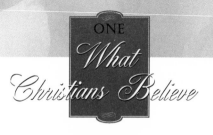

ONE
What Christians Believe

A father to the fatherless, a defender of widows, is God in his holy dwelling.
PSALM 68:5

"I believe in God the Father. . ."

The Bible teaches us that when we put our faith in God, we become children of God, and God is our Father. The dictionary defines a father as a man who begets, raises, or nurtures a child, and God is faithful to do all of those for us as His children. He created us, gives us His nature, provides for us, and loves us deeply. Some women, myself included, have gratefully experienced those things from their earthly father; but sadly, not every woman's father has lovingly raised or nurtured her. Some women have experienced their father's death, abandonment, or abuse.

It is challenging for women who haven't been cared for by their earthly fathers to understand the God of the Bible who created them, saves them, and cares for them deeply. But since injustices, large or small, cross all our paths from time to time, we are wise to realize that God's Word, not our own package of life experiences, must frame our faith.

The more we get to know God's redemptive actions in history, the greater our chances of overcoming the prison of our own narrow experience. . . .

While in practice we cannot help but be influenced in our views of God's fatherhood by our earthly experiences, the Good Father can heal our broken images.[16]

Reading God's Word helps us see that we can run to God confidently because He is our faithful Father. (Read John 10:1-30. You'll be glad you did.)

Father,
Thank You that as we read Your Word, it frames our faith and helps us to understand what a wonderful Father You are to us. Amen.

TWO

What Christians Believe

*J*oseph is a fruitful vine, a fruitful vine near a spring, whose branches climb over a wall. With bitterness archers attacked him; they shot at him with hostility. But his bow remained steady, his strong arms stayed limber, because of the hand of the Mighty One of Jacob, because of the Shepherd, the Rock of Israel, because of your father's God, who helps you, because of the Almighty, who blesses you with blessings of the heavens above, blessings of the deep that lies below, blessings of the breast and womb."
GENESIS 49:22-25

". . . Almighty . . ."

Almighty is one of the names given to God in the Old Testament (*El Shaddai*), meaning "sufficient and mighty," acknowledging God as a source of blessing. This name for God appears in the accounts of two particular Old Testament characters, Joseph and Ruth, individuals who led very difficult and trying lives.

I suppose it's not too hard to think of God as sufficient, all-powerful, and a source of blessing on sunny days when we're healthy, there's money in the checking account, and our kids are doing well. But what about the gloomy days when it feels like the rug has been pulled out from underneath us?

Joseph was left in a pit and traded for money by his brothers, taken to a foreign country, falsely accused, and sent to jail. And yet he experienced and acknowledged God's blessings—wisdom, a high position of influence, responsibility, the ability to interpret dreams, a wife and children, relief from famine, and a miraculous reunion with his brothers and father that only God could have orchestrated.

Ruth didn't have it easy either. Her husband and father-in-law died, leaving her and her mother-in-law as widows who struggled for their existence. But after Ruth chose to stay with her mother-in-law, God blessed Ruth with a husband and eventually gave them a son who became the father of King David!

The next time we face a difficult day and struggle with seeing God as sufficient, all-powerful, and full of blessing, perhaps we would be wise to read the stories of Joseph and Ruth and be encouraged anew by God's Almighty power.

Father,
Thank You that You left us with accounts of people who dealt with difficult circumstances and found Your mighty power to be more than just enough—they were blessed abundantly, and we are too. Amen.

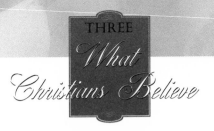

THREE

What Christians Believe

I lift up my eyes to the hills — where does my help come from? My help comes from the LORD, the Maker of heaven and earth.
PSALM 121:1-2

". . . Maker of heaven and earth . . ."

What do we do when we *make* something? If we *make* a cake, we cause it to exist by combining all the ingredients, mixing them, and then baking. If we *make* a piece of pottery, we shape some clay with our hands or a machine. If we *make* laws, we institute or establish them.

When God made heaven and earth, He introduced the wonderful process of creativity. He caused things to happen. He shaped. He established. He brought things into existence. He caused things to assume specific functions and act in specific ways.

But there's a huge difference between what we make and what God made. When we make a cake or a piece of pottery, we start with ingredients, but God made something out of nothing! I love the questions God asked Job in Job 38:4-7 (TLB): "Where were you when I laid the foundations of the earth? Tell me, if you know so much. Do you know how its dimensions were determined, and who did the surveying? What supports its foundations, and who laid its cornerstone, as the morning stars sang together and all the angels shouted for joy?" It's quite clear that God is God, and we are not!

When we encounter challenges and difficulties in our lives, how comforting and encouraging to realize that we can run to our Creator—the one who can make something out of nothing—asking Him to bring order to our sometimes chaotic existence here on earth.

Father,
Thank You that heaven and earth are full of Your glory! Thank You for creating us and giving us abilities to be creative with things that You brought into being. Amen.

What Christians Believe

Therefore, since we have been justified through faith, we have peace with God through our Lord Jesus Christ, through whom we have gained access by faith into this grace in which we now stand. And we rejoice in the hope of the glory of God.

ROMANS 5:1-2

"... and in Jesus Christ His only Son ..."

The only way to know or worship God is through belief in His Son, Jesus Christ. We might be tempted to think that a lot of people in the world know God, if the determining factor were how much they mention His name. How often we hear people exclaiming, "Thank God it's Friday!" or "For God's sake." I often wonder if people who speak God's name that way have any idea that we can know Him only through Jesus Christ. In order for *any* of us to know God, we must come to Him through *Jesus*.

> Christ is the key to knowing God ... we know God by seeing him in action, and the whole biblical story is about his action in Christ, foreshadowed in promise and accomplished in fulfillment.[17]

As we study the life, teaching, person, and work of Jesus, we learn that He has many titles—including Wonderful Counselor, the Mighty God, the Everlasting Father, and the Prince of Peace. But the three main ministries He carries out are those of prophet, priest, and king. As prophet, He reveals God's character and will to the world. As priest, instead of offering continuous animal sacrifices, He offered Himself once-for-all for the sins of the world. And as king, He is now interceding for us in heaven. God becomes known to us not as a result of what we think Him to be, but as a result of how He revealed Himself in Jesus Christ!

Father,
Thank You that when we believe in Jesus, we are reconciled to You.
Thank You that Jesus showed us the path to You. Amen.

FIVE

What Christians Believe

*Today in the town of David a Savior has been born to you;
he is Christ, the Lord."*

LUKE 2:11

". . . our Lord . . ."

When we see movies that are set in past centuries of
English history, it's not unusual to hear a subject
addressing a king as "My Lord," acknowledging a man of
renowned power or authority. Although the word *Lord* is
short, it is packed with tremendous meaning throughout
the Bible. The Old Testament word for God is translated
"Lord" in our English versions of the Bible because in late
Old Testament times Jews chose not to pronounce the
sacred name, but to say instead "my Lord." Because Jesus
taught believers to speak in a familiar way to God, we
address God by many names when we pray—Lord,
Shepherd, Redeemer, Provider, Father, and more,
stemming from the original names of God included in Old
Testament accounts.

Probably the most important name for God in the Old
Testament was Jehovah, meaning "I am who I am."

His "I am" expresses the fact that He is the infinite and original personal God who is behind everything and to whom everything must finally be traced.[18]

Other names in honor of the Lord that are included in the Old Testament are: *Jehovah-jireh* ("The Lord will provide"), *Jehovah-nissi* ("The Lord is my banner"), *Jehovah-Shalom* ("The Lord is peace"), *Jehovah-Shammah* ("The Lord is there"), *Jehovah-tsebaoth* ("The Lord of hosts"), and *Jehovah-Elohe-Yisrael* ("The Lord God of Israel").

When we address God as Lord and teach our children to address Him as Lord, we recognize Him as the only One who has infinite power to provide strength, peace, and security in our lives just as He has for others in the past.

Father,
Thank You for the honor of Your name. May we teach our children always to have great respect for You as our Lord, Shepherd, Provider, and Redeemer. Amen.

EXTRA READINGS FOR DAYS 6 AND 7
Psalm 121; Romans 5:1-11

8

What Christians Believe

PART TWO

ONE

What Christians Believe

You will be with child and give birth to a son, and you are to give him the name Jesus. He will be great and will be called the Son of the Most High. The Lord God will give him the throne of his father David, and he will reign over the house of Jacob forever; his kingdom will never end." "How will this be," Mary asked the angel, "since I am a virgin?" The angel answered, "The Holy Spirit will come upon you, and the power of the Most High will overshadow you. So the holy one to be born will be called the Son of God."

LUKE 1:31-35

". . . who was conceived by the Holy Spirit . . ."

Perhaps mothers can best understand the significance of the virgin birth of Jesus. Whether our children became part of our family through natural birth or adoption, they each had a physical father at conception. The Bible teaches us that Jesus, however, did not. Joseph became Jesus' physical father after birth, but it was God's Spirit who miraculously provided for the Son of God to enter human existence through a virgin's womb.

When Mary was visited by an angel, who explained to her that she was highly favored by God, she was very frightened until the angel told her not to be afraid—the Lord was with her. She was told that she would give birth to a son whom she was to name Jesus, and that He would be the Son of God. Mary's only question was, "How will this be, since I am a virgin?" She must have been a woman of great faith to ask "How?" Others might have said, "But this *can't* be!"

The angel went on to explain that the Holy Spirit would empower this divine, non-physical act so that Jesus, a human being, could also be called the Son of God. There's huge significance for us in the angel's words to Mary. In one of the greatest miracles of all time, Jesus was born fully God and fully man—the *only* one who could later bridge the gap between God and man!

Eternal Father,
Thank You for Your magnificent plan that brought Your love down to us. Amen.

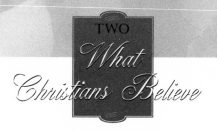

oseph son of David, do not be afraid to take Mary home as your wife,
because what is conceived in her is from the Holy Spirit.
She will give birth to a son, and you are to give him the name Jesus,
because he will save his people from their sins."
MATTHEW 1:20-21

". . . born of the virgin Mary . . ."

To think that the Creator of the universe was born of a peasant virgin on cold, hard stable ground is amazing. If I had been given the job of orchestrating Jesus' arrival on earth, I would have planned something grand. But God's designs often include humble reversals.

> It was a leap down—as if the Son of God rose from his splendor, stood poised at the rim of the universe, and dove headlong, speeding through the stars over the Milky Way to earth's galaxy, finally past Arcturus, where he plunged into a huddle of animals. . . .
>
> No child born into the world that day seemed to have lower prospects. The Son of God was born into the world not as a prince but as a pauper. We must never forget that this is where Christianity began—and where it always

begins. It begins with a sense of need, a graced sense of one's insufficiency. Christ comes to the needy. Ultimately, he is born in those who are "poor in spirit."[19]

Jesus entered the world as a servant, and that is what He asks of us—to be servants for His glory and for the increase of God's kingdom. The pattern He left for us is found in Philippians 2:5-7: "Your attitude should be the same as that of Christ Jesus: Who, being in very nature God, did not consider equality with God something to be grasped, but made himself nothing, taking the very nature of a servant, being made in human likeness."

Lord Jesus,
Forgive us for shunning humble reversals that come to our lives. Thank You that You didn't. Amen.

THREE
What Christians Believe

Christ also suffered. He died once for the sins of all us guilty sinners, although he himself was innocent of any sin at any time, that he might bring us safely home to God.

1 PETER 3:18, TLB

"... suffered under Pontius Pilate ..."

To suffer is to experience agony, distress, intense pain, or great sorrow. Ever since people chose to sin back in Genesis 3, suffering has been part of human existence. Some people suffer illness, others lose a child in an accident, some are betrayed, and others lose everything they own in a flood or a war. But Jesus experienced unparalleled suffering.

As we learn in Isaiah 53, He was despised and rejected, He carried all our sorrows, He was pierced for our transgressions, He was led like a lamb to a slaughter, and He bore the sins of the whole world. Look through a mother's eyes to get a glimpse of Jesus' suffering:

What mother's sufferings were ever equal to Mary's? Jesus was only thirty-three, her first-born, the son of her strength. There He hung before her eyes, but she was

helpless. His wounds bled, but she dared not staunch
them; His mouth was parched, but she could not moisten
it. Those outstretched arms used to clasp her neck. She
used to fondle those pierced hands and feet. Ah! The nails
pierced her as well as Him; the thorns round His brow
were a circle of flame around her heart; the taunts flung at
Him wounded her likewise.[20]

I hope I never forget that though Pilate issued the
official order sentencing Jesus to death by crucifixion,
Jesus bore the weight of all my sin as well. I deserved the
wages and penalties for my sin, and yet Jesus suffered
them for me. What a wonderful Savior!

Father,
Thank You for paying the penalty for my sin and suffering for my sin.
May I offer You my devotion in return. Amen.

What Christians Believe

And they crucified him. Dividing up his clothes, they cast lots to see what each would get.

MARK 15:24

". . . was crucified, dead, and buried . . ."

A lot of people today hang attractive crosses either on the walls of their homes or on chains around their necks. But the cross on which Jesus died was anything but attractive. During the period of history when Jesus lived, people sentenced to death on a cross were first beaten with leather lashes, often losing a great deal of blood before they were forced to carry the upper beam of their cross to the execution site. This was the case with Jesus. When the cross-beam was laid on the ground, Jesus' hands were nailed to the beam with spikes, and then his body, probably unclothed, was hoisted up. When the cross-beam was attached to a vertical stake, His feet were nailed into place.

The Jews of Jesus' time didn't believe that the world could be saved through such a bizarre plan, and many people alive today feel the same way. But God's Word teaches us that the best news the world has ever heard came from a graveyard. Jesus Christ, the sinless Son of God, died on the cross in the place of you and me, who are sinners. Before rising from the dead with eternal life, He experienced the separation from God that we deserved.

In Jesus' death on the cross we see the depth of God's love. As a result of this, men and women can be reconciled both to God and to each other.[21]

Because of His death, we have life and hope!

Father,
Thank You that because of Jesus' death on the cross, I can have a relationship with You. Thank You that I can be reconciled to others around me too because of the example and power Jesus provides for us. Amen.

FIVE

What Christians Believe

From the sixth hour until the ninth hour darkness came over all the land. About the ninth hour Jesus cried out in a loud voice, "Eloi, Eloi, lama sabachthani?" —which means, "My God, my God, why have you forsaken me?"

MATTHEW 27:45-46

". . . He descended into hell . . ."

It wasn't until I began attending a church that says the Apostle's Creed each Sunday morning that I ever gave much thought to the fact that Jesus actually experienced hell. Together with our human father, Adam, we should be the ones going to hell for our sins. The penalty for our sins should belong to us, not Jesus. But Jesus suffered for us, in our place. In order for us to experience heaven, He experienced hell. The physical torture that Jesus experienced was awful enough, but far worse for Him was the thought of becoming in His soul the sin that He hated.

He who was the truth would become the world's most inveterate liar. He who was too pure to look upon a woman to lust would become history's most promiscuous adulterer. The only man who ever loved with pure selflessness would become the most despised villain in God's universe. He would become a racist, a murderer, and gossip, slanderer, thief, and tyrant. He would become all of this not in himself, but as the sin-bearing substitute for us.[22]

Jesus spoke the words, "My God, my God, why have you forsaken me?" so that if we made a choice to believe in His provision for us, we would never have to speak those words ourselves. Jesus became God's enemy in hell so we could become God's friends, singing "Hallelujah, what a Savior!"

Father,
We can never thank You enough. "Bearing shame and scoffing rude, in my place condemned He stood—sealed my pardon with His blood: Hallelujah, what a Savior!"[23] Amen.

EXTRA READINGS FOR DAYS 6 AND 7
Matthew 1:18-25; Mark 15

9

What
Christians Believe

PART THREE

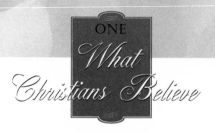

ONE

What Christians Believe

The angel said to the women, "Do not be afraid, for I know that you are looking for Jesus, who was crucified. He is not here; he has risen, just as he said. Come and see the place where he lay."

MATTHEW 28:5-6

". . . the third day He rose again from the dead . . ."

The resurrection of Jesus is the capstone of all His teaching and ministry, proving to the disciples and to us that He really is the Son of God. The classic pictures of the Resurrection in our mind are a stone rolled away from the entrance to Jesus' tomb, grave-clothes left behind, an earthquake, and an angel speaking to the women at the tomb. In contrast to the crucifixion account where everything appeared to be coming to a grinding halt with Jesus' death, His resurrection was surrounded by a frenzy of activity that included Jesus' friends running back and forth in breathless excitement.

Without the Resurrection our Christian beliefs and hopes would be meaningless, because our lives can be transformed only by the same power that overcame evil and death and raised Christ from the dead! Because Jesus was raised from the dead, just as He and the Scriptures both promised, we can believe that He will accomplish everything else He has promised us in His Word.

Even Jesus' disciples struggled at first with understanding His resurrection, and people today are no different. Some first think the Resurrection to be a fairy tale but are willing to examine it further. If we are serious about wanting to know the truth, we will eventually encounter Jesus personally; and as we enter into a personal relationship with Him, we begin to experience His power to change our lives.

Father,
Thank You that because of Jesus' resurrection we have hope both for this life and for eternity. Thank You that the power that raised Jesus from the grave is the same power that changes us and helps us as we trust in You. Amen.

TWO

What Christians Believe

When he had led them out to the vicinity of Bethany, he lifted up his hands and blessed them. While he was blessing them, he left them and was taken up into heaven. Then they worshiped him and returned to Jerusalem with great joy. And they stayed continually at the temple, praising God.
LUKE 24:50-53

". . . He ascended into heaven . . ."

I find it reassuring that Jesus remained on earth for forty days after His resurrection to minister to His disciples. The official Jewish position in reaction to the Resurrection was that Jesus wasn't alive—they said His disciples had just stolen Jesus' dead body. So it was very important that the disciples be able to refute that lie to the people. The disciples' spiritual power was dependent on Jesus' resurrection, because if Jesus had remained dead, there would have been no message of hope.

Some people may wonder why Jesus went back to heaven, but if He hadn't, the Holy Spirit would not have come to the believer's hearts. Jesus assured His disciples that the Holy Spirit would give ordinary believers extraordinary power through His work in their lives.

Before Jesus' death and resurrection, the disciples had worried too much about the positions, privileges, and politics of God's kingdom, but after the Resurrection Jesus spoke to them about what was most important—the coming of God's kingdom to people's *hearts*.

Other aspects of Jesus' ministry that began after His ascension were intercession and forgiveness, which are huge gifts to us as believers. Jesus intercedes for us to God, petitioning God on our behalf and bringing us into relationship with God as a result of our faith in Him. He's also our advocate before the Father, offering forgiveness when we confess our sins.

The Savior who was spat on, humiliated, and crucified on the cross was lifted up to the heavens and now prays for us and offers us forgiveness!

Father,
Thank You for the reassurance You gave to the disciples after Jesus' resurrection, and thanks for the reassurance we have today of the presence of Your Spirit in our lives. Thank You that because Jesus ascended to You, He intercedes on our behalf! Amen.

*That power is like the working of his mighty strength, which he exerted
in Christ when he raised him from the dead and seated him at
his right hand in the heavenly realms, far above all rule and
authority, power and dominion, and every title that can be given,
not only in the present age but also in the one to come.*
EPHESIANS 1:19-21

". . . and sitteth on the right hand of God the Father
almighty . . ."

Although Jesus had remained silent throughout His
trial before the crucifixion, He did answer one of the high
priest's questions: "'Tell us if you are the Christ, the Son of
God.' 'Yes, it is as you say,' Jesus replied. 'But I say to all
of you: In the future you will see the Son of Man sitting at
the right hand of the Mighty One and coming on the clouds
of heaven'" (Matthew 26:63-64).

This declaration of Jesus holds great meaning for *our*
personal faith. We know that He has already ascended to
sit at the right hand of God, but *in the same breath* He said
He would come on the clouds of heaven—a great promise
to us that He is coming back!

What is the significance of Jesus sitting at the right hand of God the Father?

In the ancient world, the emperor would sometimes seal the treaty between his empire and a lesser kingdom by a regal ceremony in which the local king would take his place at the right hand of the emperor, the place of power and authority. Thus, he would be adopted in a sense by the great king as a son.[24]

Not only does Jesus sit at the right hand of the Father, but *we will reign with Him* if we have put our faith in Him. "For if, by the trespass of the one man, death reigned through that one man, how much more will those who receive God's abundant provision of grace and of the gift of righteousness reign in life through the one man, Jesus Christ" (Romans 5:17).

Father,
Thanks that Your mighty strength that raised Jesus from the dead and seated Him at Your right hand is the same power You share with us to enable us to lead a victorious life. Amen.

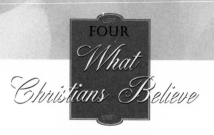

But now he has appeared once for all at the end of the ages to do away with sin by the sacrifice of himself. Just as man is destined to die once, and after that to face judgment, so Christ was sacrificed once to take away the sins of many people; and he will appear a second time, not to bear sin, but to bring salvation to those who are waiting for him.
HEBREWS 9:26-28

". . . from thence He shall come to judge the living and the dead . . ."

The time to experience God's mercy is now. Since Jesus died and rose again, victorious over sin and death, the devil's plans to thwart salvation were destroyed. Satan knows he's lost the war, but he still wants to take people down with him. The good news is that we have a choice. Through faith in Christ we can be saved from death and hell. We can follow Christ, saying to Him, "Your will be done" through our faith and obedient living. Or we can be unrepentant sinners who through lack of faith in Christ and living in disobedience to His teaching say, "My will be done."

Those who choose faith in Christ and obedience to His

teaching will reign with Him in heaven forever. But those who don't make that choice will experience the inescapable torments of hell—separation from all hope, love, peace, and joy.

> Thus, our Redeeming King has ascended to heaven for this two-fold purpose; to secure the everlasting safety of his people, and to execute everlasting judgment against those who do not receive him. It is good news for all who will believe, but the worst possible news for those who go on in their ignorance, apathy, and rebellion. Christ is now in heaven and he will return. Will we be among those reconciled sinners who love his appearing? Or will we be among those who are caught in terror?[25]

If our faith in Christ bears evidence of repentance and obedience in our lives, we need not fear!

Father,
Thank You for Your justice and Your mercy. Thank You that as we come to You in faith, You surround us with Your mercy, and we need have no fear of judgment. Amen.

FIVE

What Christians Believe

*B*ut the Counselor, the Holy Spirit, whom the Father will send
in my name, will teach you all things and will remind you
of everything I have said to you."

JOHN 14:26

". . . I believe in the Holy Spirit . . ."

The Holy Spirit, one of the three members of the
Godhead, has the role of communication and connection
between people and God. As we spend time in God's Word,
the Holy Spirit comes alongside us to plant truth in our
minds, convince us of God's will, and point out where we
are straying from it.

Theologians use the term illumination to describe the
Holy Spirit's process of helping believers understand
Scripture. Without God, sinful people are unable to
recognize and obey divine truths. When a person is
reborn, the Holy Spirit helps the person to see God's
Word with the eyes of faith and love. The Holy Spirit also
works in the life of the believer, convincing him of the
truth of the Bible, keeping him from misconstruing what
it really says, and helping him not be distracted so he can
see and remember the true meaning of God's Word.[26]

Counselor was one of many titles given to Christ, and after we come to faith in Christ, God's Holy Spirit becomes our counselor, adviser, and guide. Because there is nothing He does not know, He is the supreme counselor.

Because the Holy Spirit is the power by which believers come to Christ and see with new eyes of faith, He is closer to us than we are to ourselves.[27]

The Holy Spirit is the most qualified counselor in the universe because He knows us, loves us, encourages us, is patient with us, and prays for us. How thankful we are for His presence in our lives!

Father,
Thank You that the Holy Spirit knows us better than we know ourselves. Please counsel us in Your ways and give us Your guidance and help. Amen.

EXTRA READINGS FOR DAYS 6 AND 7
Matthew 28:1-15; Luke 24:36-53

10

What Christians Believe

PART FOUR

ONE
What Christians Believe

*And God placed all things under his feet and appointed him to be
head over everything for the church, which is his body,
the fullness of him who fills everything in every way.*
EPHESIANS 1:22

"... the holy catholic Church ..."

One Sunday when a friend was worshiping with our family at College Church (in Wheaton, Illinois), she leaned over and asked, "Since this isn't a Catholic church, why does the Apostle's Creed say, 'I believe in one holy catholic Church'?" I briefly explained that the word *catholic* means general, worldwide, or universal, as opposed to specific. The Bible teaches that Jesus calls the church His *bride* and that the universal church includes all believers, gathered under the head of Christ. Being united with other believers is not something *we* do—Christ has already accomplished it! We are miraculously united to other believers because God has united us to His Son. The church is not our idea but God's!

What a consolation it is for us to know that our Savior could think of nothing else before he went to the cross than the salvation, blessing and joy of his church. If he had the good of his bride in view when he was about to suffer divine wrath for her sins, then surely he seeks only her welfare in heaven now as he enjoys his eternal reign in victory.[28]

The church is both visible and invisible. God alone knows the hearts of all the people in *visible* churches around the world. We do not know who in their innermost beings worships Him and who does not. He sees the *invisible* church—those who love Him and obey Him; and He uses the visible church to spread His Good News and build up the faith of His children.

Father,
Thank You that even in heaven Jesus prays for Your church here on earth—for our joy, protection, purity, and unity. May we be faithful members of Your invisible church, no matter where we worship and serve You visibly. Amen.

I have given them the glory that you gave me, that they may be one
as we are one: I in them and you in me. May they be brought
to complete unity to let the world know that you sent me and
have loved them even as you have loved me."
JOHN 17:22-23

". . . the communion of saints . . ."

The communion of saints is the fellowship of believers—
past, present, and future—who share a relationship with
Christ and thus with each other. As we raise our children,
it's important to teach them that the community of saints is
not just the believers who are alive in our little *visible* church
body, but that it's a *historical* community. We learn much
from the heroes of the Bible and heroes of past ages, and
they give us roots and accountability—two things sadly
lacking in our society today.

Not only are we bound with the church of other times, but
to the church of other places. This is sometimes forgotten,
especially when we confuse our nation with the Kingdom
of God. Is the church an American institution, or is it a
heavenly kingdom? Is it a kingdom of political power, one

of the imperial layers of the statue in Nebuchadnezzar's dream, or is it the Kingdom of grace whose borders reach across time and place? . . . we are more related to Christians in China, Africa, the Middle East, and Russia than we are to our own neighbors—even those with conservative moral values—who are not in union with Christ and His church.[29]

The communion of saints is not based on church denomination, intelligence level, economic status, or personality type. Our fellowship is centered on Christ. Colossians 3:11(TLB) says, "In this new life one's nationality or race or education or social position is unimportant; such things mean nothing. Whether a person has Christ is what matters, and he is equally available to all."

Father,
What a privilege it is to be united with Your body of believers—Your church! Thank You that when we get to heaven one day, we'll be praising You with people from many different countries and languages. Thank You that our communion is possible because of Christ's death on the cross for us. Amen.

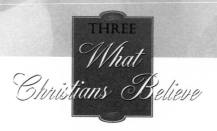

THREE

What Christians Believe

*If you, O LORD, kept a record of sins, O LORD, who could stand?
But with you there is forgiveness; therefore you are feared.*

PSALM 130:3-4

". . . the forgiveness of sins . . ."

Forgiveness is man's deepest need and God's highest achievement.

HORACE BUSHNELL

The story is told in Spain of a father and his teenage son who had a relationship that had become strained. So the son ran away from home. His father, however, began a journey in search of his rebellious son. Finally, in Madrid, in a last desperate effort to find him, the father put an ad in the newspaper. The ad read: "Dear Paco, meet me in front of the newspaper office at noon. All is forgiven. I love you. Your father." The next day at noon in front of the newspaper office 800 Pacos showed up, all seeking forgiveness and love from their fathers.

The Bible is the only religious book that teaches that God completely forgives sins. Although God says sin deserves punishment because it violates His holy character, He is also a God of grace and pardon who *initiates* forgiveness.

Before God can forgive sin, two conditions must be present. There needs to be a blood sacrifice, and a person must have a repentant heart. In Old Testament times, animal sacrifices were made over and over to cover sin, pointing ahead to Christ. And when Jesus came, He became a once-for-all sacrifice—the just for the unjust.

Before we meet Christ, we are all Pacos needing to meet our fathers in front of the newspaper office. But the beauty of Christ's forgiveness is that we can receive it anytime and anywhere, as long as we have seen our sin and trust in His blood!

Father,
Thank You so much for Your complete forgiveness. May our lives show how much we appreciate Your amazing gift to us. Amen.

FOUR

What Christians Believe

*Listen, I tell you a mystery: We will not all sleep, but we will
all be changed—in a flash, in the twinkling of an eye,
at the last trumpet. For the trumpet will sound,
the dead will be raised imperishable, and we will be changed.*

1 CORINTHIANS 15:51-52

". . . the resurrection of the body . . ."

I wish that as part of today's reading I could enclose a CD or audio cassette of Handel's *Messiah*—specifically, the bass recitative and solo of "The Trumpet Shall Sound." Being a musician, I get goose bumps when I hear that piece; the marriage of the biblical text to the music creates strong feelings of anticipation. (If you have a recording at home, listen to it with your Bible open to 1 Corinthians 15, and get ready for a meaningful worship experience!)

In order to explain the resurrection of the dead, Paul used the picture of a seed. When a seed of any kind is sown in the ground, it first dies and then rises as something much more beautiful than the seed. The same is true of the caterpillar, which becomes a butterfly—helpful in explaining the resurrection to a child. So it is with our bodies too. They are sown perishable, but they are raised imperishable. They are sown as natural bodies, but they are raised as spiritual bodies.

So what does all that mean to us *today*? It's sobering to realize that *every* human being who ever lived in a human body will have an eternal spiritual body. But the question is, what kind? Those who have trusted and obeyed Christ will have heavenly bodies, and those who have turned their backs on Christ will have bodies suited to their environment in hell.

If we believe what the Bible teaches us about the resurrection, we will want to use our bodies today to the glory of God!

A Prayer of Hope:
"So, my dear brothers, since future victory is sure, be strong and steady, always abounding in the Lord's work, for you know that nothing you do for the Lord is ever wasted as it would be if there were no resurrection" (1 Corinthians 15:58, TLB).

FIVE

What Christians Believe

Since, then, you have been raised with Christ, set your hearts on things above, where Christ is seated at the right hand of God. Set your mind on things above, not on earthly things. For you died, and your life is now hidden with Christ in God. When Christ, who is your life, appears, then you also will appear with him in glory.

COLOSSIANS 3:1-4

" . . . and the life everlasting . . ."

It would be incorrect for us to think that everlasting life begins only when our bodies die. For the person who trusts Christ as their Savior, everlasting life begins *immediately*, giving us a portfolio of riches that some Christians don't realize they have available to them.

This is the cycle: The Law leads us to despair so that we flee to Christ. Once united to Christ, we bear fruit, since we share corporately in his Resurrection Life. Then our joy in the present realities of the age of the Spirit becomes an opportunity for our sinful hearts to regain self-confidence. We need to hear the Law again, judging our best works, so that we will flee to Christ. We also need to be reminded that it is the intrusion of the coming age into the present, not the gradual improvement of the sinful nature, that is responsible for our new life and growth in Christ.[30]

When we first put our faith in Christ, we become a new creation. God tells us that the old passes, and the new comes. God's Word guides us into truth, and the presence of His Spirit is our down payment. So we don't have to wait for physical death or the Rapture before we experience everlasting life. Our faith in Christ makes it a present reality!

Father,
Thanks that the everlasting life You give is something we begin to experience as soon as we trust Christ. Thanks that we receive Your Spirit as a down payment. Amen.

EXTRA READINGS FOR DAYS 6 AND 7
John 17:20-26; Psalm 130

11

Witness

ONE *Witness*

"Hear, O Israel: The LORD our God, the LORD is one. Love the LORD your God with all your heart and with all your soul and with all your strength. These commandments that I give you today are to be upon your hearts. Impress them on your children. Talk about them when you sit at home and when you walk along the road, when you lie down and when you get up."

DEUTERONOMY 6:4-7

The second of my three sons was baptized last night. As I listened to the testimonies of the seven junior and senior high school students who were baptized, I was struck by how many times the students said their *mothers* were the ones who introduced them to Jesus—and the majority of those related that it happened at bedtime, when the moms were tucking the children in for the night.

It's no surprise to us moms that our children often open up about things that are on their hearts and minds during those closing moments of the day. They don't feel the rush of getting to the next activity, and as we sit on the bed or snuggle with them, they are often interested in extending the moments of closeness.

In order for us to be effective witnesses for God in the lives of our children, several things have to happen. First, we need to listen to God through His Word and through prayer. Second, we choose *ourselves* to love God with all our heart, soul, and strength. Third, we open our hearts to God, exchanging our sinful ways for His righteous ways. Fourth, we make a conscious effort to impress God's Word on our children's hearts, realizing this can happen in many different settings and postures.

As we listen to God, open our hearts to God, and share His Word with our children, we eagerly await evidences of faith and growth in their hearts.

Father,
Thank You for the great privilege of pointing and leading our children to You. May we not cause our children to stumble by failing to walk closely with You ourselves. Amen.

TWO

Witness

We are therefore Christ's ambassadors, as though God were making his appeal through us. We implore you on Christ's behalf: Be reconciled to God.

2 CORINTHIANS 5:20

When I visit Washington D.C. I like to drive past embassies of ambassadors from other countries. The architectural designs of the buildings reflect the countries that are represented.

Ambassadors are diplomatic officers of high rank who represent one nation in the capital of another, skillfully reporting on matters of their government. Although bound by instructions and beliefs from their homeland, ambassadors exercise considerable authority with discretion. In order for ambassadors to be effective, they must act acceptably in the receiving country.

When we enter into a relationship with God, we too become ambassadors with a message. As mothers, we are ambassadors first to our children, and they live in the embassy along with us—the embassy of our home. If God's Spirit is present in our lives, they will see whom we represent. The message we have been given is that through Christ we can have a relationship with God. When man rebelled against God, we became His enemies, but God provided a way for us to be forgiven through Jesus' death on the cross. When we see our need for God, desire a relationship with Him, and turn to Christ, He takes away our guilt and gives us His righteousness.

Our responsibility is to represent God as tactfully as we can because we are messengers of peace. Our daily briefing on God's plan for the world comes through the time we spend in His Word. We represent the King of kings, and our homes are embassies. What a privileged position we hold!

God,
Thank You that You have chosen us to represent You. May we do it with accurate information and tact that come from You. Amen.

THREE

Witness

*ut in your hearts set apart Christ as Lord. Always be prepared
to give an answer to everyone who asks you to give the reason
for the hope that you have.*

1 PETER 3:15

While walking with my friend Ruthie one morning, she related something that had happened the day before. She had been to see her regular hairdresser for a trim, when the hairdresser asked, "What makes you the way you are? You live a charming life, although I know you encounter difficult things like everybody else. But you're cheerful, and you don't bad-mouth other people. So what's different about you?"

First, Ruthie laughed and jokingly suggested, "I must be blessed with lots of serotonin in my blood!" Then she offered, "My life is different because of my relationship with Jesus Christ." Her hairdresser responded that she suspected it would have something to do with religion. Ruthie later followed through on that initial question, and seeds of truth are being planted. I came away from my walk with Ruthie reminded that people outside of God's kingdom notice attractive qualities in those who are part of God's kingdom.

Each spring break my family vacations on the beach in Florida where we spend a whole week in the sun. Upon our return to Illinois, friends often ask, "Where have you been? It must have been somewhere warm!" When we spend lots of time with God's *Son*, in prayer and in God's Word, people will notice that too. Our lives will be different. They will see the attractive fruits of God's Spirit and find hope.

Father,
Thank You that we are encouraged when people who don't know You notice there's something different about people who do. May we walk closely to You in obedience, so we will never be a disgrace to Your kingdom. Amen.

FOUR

Witness

I pray that you may be active in sharing your faith, so that you will have a full understanding of every good thing we have in Christ.

PHILEMON 6

If our life is built on a vertical relationship with Christ, we will be motivated to move outward horizontally, bearing witness of that relationship to others. To be an effective communicator of our faith to those around us, we need to have knowledge and perception of the good things we have in Christ.

Colossians 3:12-17 is a passage of Scripture that reminds us what the "wardrobe" of the Christian in-cludes—the virtues that develop as we walk with Jesus.

1. "Compassion"—tender hearts.

2. "Kindness"—thoughtfulness, understanding, and generosity.

3. "Humility"—lack of pride and pretentiousness.

4. "Gentleness"—a mild and pleasant nature.

5. "Patience"—a willingness to endure.

6. "Forbearance"—bearing with one another.

7. "Forgiveness"—after dealing with our complaints, we stop blaming each other.

138

8. "Love"—being devoted to one another, thus bringing unity and wholeness.

9. "Peace"—being in harmony with each other.

10. "Thankfulness"—gratefulness and appreciation.

11. Love for God's Word—allowing it to dwell in our hearts, and then wanting to share it with others.

12. A desire to please Jesus. Warren Wiersbe says, "What blessings would come to our homes if each member of the family said, 'I will live each day to please Christ and make Him preeminent in all things.' There would be less selfishness and more love; less impatience and more tenderness; less wasting of money on foolish things and more living for the things that matter most."

These are the garments of our wardrobe that bear witness to those around us that we know Christ!

Father,
Just as we spend time taking care of our wardrobe and the wardrobes of our family members, may we spend time with You, through Your Word and prayer, so that the garments of our hearts will point a watching world to You. Amen.

FIVE

Witness

As Jesus was walking beside the Sea of Galilee, he saw two brothers, Simon called Peter and his brother Andrew. They were casting a net into the lake, for they were fishermen. "Come, follow me," Jesus said, "and I will make you fishers of men."

MATTHEW 4:18-19

"Fishers of men" was not used for the first time in the Bible. Used for centuries by Greek and Roman philosophers, the phrase described a person seeking to "catch" others through teaching and persuasion. Since the men involved in this account in Matthew's Gospel were fishermen, it made a lot of sense for Jesus to use the analogy.

On our vacation at the ocean this past summer, one activity some of the males in the family enjoyed was fishing. Before our vacation the guys checked out a few books on fishing from the library, which I browsed through one morning. After glancing through one of those books, I realized that there really *is* an art to fishing. It requires skill and knowledge, and the person who catches the most fish is probably the one who knows which fishing tackle to use, how to present the bait, where to find the fish, and how to

go after them. No one ever becomes perfect at fishing—
there's always something new to be learned.

People who do serious fishing are courageous and
patient people. They are also people who need faith,
because they don't see the fish and they are never exactly
sure what they will encounter. Here's how Warren Wiersbe
describes New Testament fishermen:

> They had been catching living fish and, when they caught
> them, the fish died. Now they would catch dead fish—
> sinners—and the fish would live![31]

If fishing for fish takes skill, patience, courage,
knowledge, and faith, how much more so does fishing for
men!

God,
Thank You for pictures in Your Word that point out some of our
responsibilities as believers. Please help us to be concerned for the souls
of people who don't know You. Amen.

EXTRA READINGS FOR DAYS 6 AND 7
Matthew 5:13-16; Deuteronomy 6

12

Praise

ONE

Praise

I will extol the LORD at all times; his praise will always be on my lips.
PSALM 34:1

It's important for us to teach our children that praising and worshiping God doesn't happen only on Sundays when we're sitting or singing in church, but that praising God ought to happen throughout each day. Taking a walk in the spring and admiring the daffodils is an experience that prompts our praise, whether we do it at that moment or wait until bedtime to talk to God.

My eleven-year-old and I praised God last night when we received happy news of another cousin born into the family. When we visit the new baby and parents in Des Moines, Iowa, later this week, it will be a worshipful experience for me. Holding a new baby in my arms is always cause for praise that God continues the cycle of life.

Reading a book on the universe together with a child is another experience that stimulates our praise. A book I enjoyed reading with my children was *Spinning Worlds*—a child's guide to God's creation in the heavens. Does your child know that:

- God covered the earth with a substance not found anywhere else in the whole solar system. (Liquid water.)
- One million earths could fit inside the sun.
- God made the sun the perfect distance from the earth, so that it gives us just the right amounts of heat and light. If it were too close, we would die from heat; if it were too far away, we'd perish from the cold.

If we regularly praise God for His creations and provisions, our example may prompt our children to do the same.

Father,
Throughout the day, as we notice something that You made or something You have done, may we remember to praise You for it. Amen.

TWO

Praise

O Lord our God, the majesty and glory of your name fills all the earth and overflows the heavens.

PSALM 8:1, TLB

Imagine you are the creator and founder of a very large catering company. Not only did you form the company, but you personally crafted all the recipes being prepared and served. You selected, hired, and trained the entire staff, teaching them exactly how the food would be prepared and how the company would operate. Your company is seen as such a success that you have been invited to a convention where your employees will prepare and serve the food.

At the convention, as the food is prepared and served, everyone exclaims how delicious and well-presented the meal is. In the talk after the meal, all the ingredients are analyzed and the methods of preparation discussed, but no one ever acknowledges you as the creator, developer, and overseer of the company. You leave the event without having been recognized or affirmed by anyone—even your own staff!

I sometimes wonder if that's the way God feels when we

go to the zoo and see all the animals He has created but forget to acknowledge Him. I wonder how God feels when we walk outside late at night to observe the heavens, admiring the beauty of the moon and stars, but forget to praise Him for designing and sustaining such beauty and glory. The next time we're admiring some of God's creation with our children, let's be sure and call attention to the Creator and give honor to Him.

Father,
May I not be slow to see and praise Your handiwork as I encounter it many times throughout each day. Amen.

THREE

Praise

Praise the LORD. How good it is to sing praises to our God, how pleasant and fitting to praise him!
PSALM 147:1

I've been reading a lot about heaven recently. Consequently I've also been reading about praise, because that's what happens continuously in heaven—now and forever. Sometimes I think of heaven as an escape from pain, disappointment, work, or schedules, and I am thankful that we'll be done with all of the above when we get there. But heaven is much more than deliverance from problems—we'll be in God's presence and will enjoy and praise Him forever. Forever is a very long time. I remember trying to understand the word *eternity* as a child and getting quite frustrated. Each time I'd think about it, I'd think to myself, "But there *has* to be an end!"

If I'm going to praise God continuously in heaven, I need more practice doing it here on earth. In my devotional time early this morning, I read Psalm 150:1-6:

> *Praise the LORD. Praise God in his sanctuary; praise him in his mighty heavens. Praise him for his acts of power; praise him for*

his surpassing greatness. Praise him with the sounding of the trumpet, praise him with the harp and lyre, praise him with tambourine and dancing, praise him with the strings and flute, praise him with the clash of cymbals, praise him with resounding cymbals. Let everything that has breath praise the LORD. Praise the LORD.

After reading the psalm, I was prompted to do two things. The first was to read the verse about praising God with the sound of the trumpet to my eleven-year-old son, who was going to be playing his trumpet in band today. The second was to take a walk outside after the children left for school and, while I walked, praise God. By the time I arrived back home, my heart was joyful, and I realized that praising God makes us feel full of Him—as we *always* will in heaven!

God of forever,
We have so much to praise You for. May we practice praising You regularly on earth since we will be doing it forever in heaven. Amen.

FOUR

Praise

*et the name of the LORD be praised, both now and forevermore.
From the rising of the sun to the place where it sets, the name
of the LORD is to be praised.*

PSALM 113:2-3

I'm not real great with geography, but when I check into a
hotel that has clocks on the wall showing time zones in
different countries of the world, I'm fascinated. I also enjoy
looking at my world atlas and realizing that when it's 6 A.M.
in Chicago, it's 6 P.M. in Singapore, and it's 10 P.M. in
Sydney, Australia.

One of the pastors in my church was extending the call
to worship in a Sunday morning service recently, and after
he read the verse above, he pointed out that because the
sun is always rising somewhere over the earth each hour,
God is receiving praise from His people constantly! I get
goose bumps just thinking about that. First someone in
Chicago, then New York, then Halifax, then Rio de
Janeiro, then Nairobi, and the list of cities continues, as

does the praise. Of course, the angels praise God without end in heaven.

Christians are not the only people who can bring some justice into the world. They are not the only people who can add to the world's art or philosophy. They are not the only people who put out newsletters and go to committee meetings and play in bowling leagues. But they are the only ones who praise Jesus Christ.[32]

Praise is unique to Christians, and as long as we have breath we are privileged to be able to praise God!

Father,
May I praise You more! Amen.

FIVE

Praise

*O Lord, what a variety you have made! And in wisdom you have
made them all! The earth is full of your riches.*
PSALM 104:24, TLB

Early this morning I praised God while I watched a sand
crab. I had just completed an early morning walk along the
oceanfront where my family is vacationing, and as I was
sitting in the sand, I noticed some movement out of the
corner of my eye. Looking closer, I discovered a sand crab
about four or five inches in diameter with two beady eyes
sticking up from the rest of its body.

Sand crabs are cute little critters that science fiction
producers have copied for some of their movies! The sand
crab I was watching came up out of its hole, pushed some
sand out, and then sat there awhile looking at me,
eventually going back underground. The routine was
repeated several more times until I got up to leave. As I
watched the sand crab, I thought about how many
fascinating creatures God has created. Since I am a finite
creature, I can only be in one place at a time to enjoy His
creation. The creatures I could see this morning included

sand crabs, jellyfish, and seagulls. But God is omnipresent, able to be everywhere at once; so He can see all the creatures in the world *at the same time!*

When I praise God for how wonderful and big He is, my perspective changes. I'm reminded how dependent I am on Him, and I'm also reminded that if He is big enough to have created and sustained the sand crab in Gulf Shores, Alabama, the giraffe in Tanzania, and the panda in China, He's big enough to take care of me.

God,
Thank You that You can be everywhere at once, watching over all Your
creation, and still care about me. May this encourage me to run to You
anytime, anywhere. Amen.

EXTRA READINGS FOR DAYS 6 AND 7
Psalm 103; Psalm 113

13

Reverence

ONE

Reverence

Therefore, since we are receiving a kingdom that cannot be shaken, let us be thankful, and so worship God acceptably with reverence and awe, for our God is a consuming fire.
HEBREWS 12:28-29

Reverence is a word we don't hear very often anymore. Maybe people today think the word sounds a bit archaic — a word from the past. The essence of true reverence is to treasure God in our hearts and to think about Him often.

When God chose Mary to be Jesus' mother, He didn't choose her for her impressive experience as a mom, because she had none. But she had a great reverence toward God. When she sang about what God was doing in her life, she said, "His mercy extends to those who fear him, from generation to generation" (Luke 1:50).

When Diana, Princess of Wales, was interviewed several years before she died, her life appeared to be quite a contrast with Mary's. Diana was wealthy, and Mary was poor. Diana had a royal, fairy-tale wedding that was watched around the world by about 750 million people. Mary waited in seclusion after the angel's announcement.

In Diana's interview, she said she wanted to be "queen of people's hearts." Mary said she wanted to be a handmaiden of the Lord—His servant.

A *Chicago Tribune* article from August 31, 1997, stated, "The Princess of Wales was beautiful, famous and wealthy, and she won the admiration of millions, but she found simple happiness elusive." Mary led a simple life with difficult circumstances, but she had lasting joy and blessing.

What an example Mary left for us as mothers. May we treasure God in our hearts and think about Him often. Reverence is not an archaic word—it's a word for today!

God,
Thank You for Mary's example of a reverent life. Please help me treasure You in my heart and think about You often. Amen.

TWO

Reverence

He who fears the LORD has a secure fortress, and for his children it will be a refuge.
PROVERBS 14:26

The benefits of reverence for God don't stop with us—they are passed down to our children in some very unique ways. We're taught here that if a parent reverences the Lord, he or she has a secure spiritual fortress, and the refuge and protection of that fortress will be experienced by his or her children as well. Let's take a closer look.

A fortress includes walls around a city to protect that city from enemy attacks. Back in Bible times these walls were fifteen to twenty-five feet thick and twenty-five feet high. On top of these walls, towers were built at regular intervals, giving the people defending the city a good viewpoint from which they could counter an attack. The outside walls were protected by a moat that made direct assault almost impossible. Cities inside a fortress typically had only one gate—two at the most—keeping security very tight. Since no city could last long without an adequate water supply, fortified cities were generally built near rivers or springs.

When we choose to reverence God by trusting Him, spending time in His Word, and obeying what we're learning, our walls are built thick, we become wise as to what we need to look out for, and our water supply is unending. Even if a mom did not experience growing up in a family fortress of faith and security, she can choose, through reverence for God, to have that security for herself and for her children.

Father,
Thank You that You want to be our fortress. May we choose to reverence You so we will experience security for ourselves and for our children. Amen.

THREE

Reverence

When it was almost time for the Jewish Passover, Jesus went up to Jerusalem. In the temple courts he found men selling cattle, sheep and doves, and others sitting at tables exchanging money. So he made a whip out of cords, and drove all from the temple area, both sheep and cattle; he scattered the coins of the money changers and overturned their tables.

JOHN 2:13-15

Reverence isn't always quiet. Sometimes a display of reverence is rather surprising to those who are watching.

In Old Testament times God had instructed Israelites to bring their best animals for sacrifice. In New Testament times the temple priests developed a market for buying sacrificial animals—they knew it was difficult for pilgrims to bring their animals on the long journey to Jerusalem. But what began as a local farmer's market on the way to Jerusalem became a big, dishonest business that took up lots of space on the temple grounds. With all the hustle and bustle of this dishonest and greedy business taking place in the temple, it was difficult to worship, which was what they were all supposed to be doing.

These greedy businessmen were making a mockery of God's house of worship, and because Jesus was zealous for the reverence of God, He displayed His reverence in a less-than-quiet manner.

He made a whip—a deliberate and forceful response.

He drove the money changers away. However, this was not out-of-control loss of temper. His actions expressed anger, but He was clearly in control.

He said, "Get out of here." Jesus' reverence for God prompted Him to meet mockery of God with serious consequences.

We often think of reverence as quiet, and many times it is. But there are times in our lives when our reverence for God prompts us to meet mockery of God with actions that are deliberately and carefully enforced.

Father,
May we be zealous about not wanting to do or give way to anything that would be mockery of You. Amen.

FOUR

Reverence

The fear of the LORD is the beginning of knowledge,
but fools despise wisdom and discipline.
PROVERBS 1:7

It's the day after Christmas, and while paging through the morning newspaper, I stopped to read an article titled "Nativity Spoof in Need of Seasonal Forgiveness." To say that I was saddened by the article would be much too mild. Here's an excerpt:

> "We hope God has a sense of humor," declares the program to *The Madonna In Spite of Herself,* Corn Production's new late-night musical Nativity spoof, "or else we're in a lot of trouble." No kidding. Given that this fringe Chicago troupe translates [the Virgin] Mary into a big-haired gum-chomping resident of Berwyn, Joseph (a.k.a. Joey) into a genial sexual predator, and the Angel Gabriel into a screaming vamp in a hot outfit, the youthful satirists at Corn Productions had better hope for some Christian forgiveness and seasonal goodwill. Otherwise, they'll have a lot more to worry about than lumps of coal in their collective stockings.[33]

After reading the depressing article, I wondered what each person involved in the production had learned about the birth of Christ as a child. Had they heard Luke 2 read at home with reverence? Had they been part of a loving body of believers where the account of Jesus' birth was portrayed respectfully? Had they ever had the chance to sense, deep in their souls, the beauty of the greatest story ever told?

What a great opportunity we moms have, while our children are living in our home, to sow seeds of respect for God and His Word!

Father,
Thanks for moments that jolt us into remembering that what we think of You is not to be taken lightly. What we think about You affects the way we live. May we show You great reverence and by our examples and words encourage our children to reverence You. Amen.

FIVE

Reverence

Serve the Lord with reverent fear.
PSALM 2:11, TLB

"Reverent fear" —now that's an interesting word combination! Let's look closely at each of the two words.

Reverence —"a feeling of profound awe and respect. Because of His majesty and holiness, God arouses a feeling of reverence in those who worship and serve Him."[34]

Fear —"a feeling of reverence, awe, and respect, *or* an unpleasant emotion caused by a sense of danger. Fear may be directed toward God or humankind, and it may be either healthy or harmful."[35]

"Reverent fear," for the Christian, is not a harmful fear that includes a sense of terror or dread. In God's Word, Christians are taught not to fear other humans, because people cannot touch our souls. But the Bible also teaches that wicked people do fear others, acting deceitfully as they attempt to hide their sins. Unbelievers have every reason to fear God as well because they stand condemned before Him. This is usually not the kind of fear that leads them to repentance. Quite the opposite; the unbeliever tries to hide from God, until he or she gets a glimpse of God's love and grace.

But healthy fear includes reverence and respect. Proverbs 9:10 teaches that "the fear of the LORD is the beginning of wisdom." All of our work, all of our actions, and all of our service to God must come from a heart that has a profound sense of awe and respect for Him. May our children see that in our lives, so they will want to serve the Lord respectfully themselves.

Father,
May we treat You with the reverence You so deserve. When we experience Your love and grace, we want to do that. Please help us model reverence for You to our children. Amen.

EXTRA READINGS FOR DAYS 6 AND 7
John 2:12-25; Psalm 2

1. F. B. Meyer, *F. B. Meyer Bible Commentary* (Wheaton, Ill.: Tyndale House, 1984), p. 478.

2. "Near to the Heart of God," *The Worshiping Church Hymnal* (Carol Stream, Ill.: Hope Publishing Company, 1990), p. 542.

3. R. Kent Hughes, *1,001 Great Stories & Quotes* (Wheaton, Ill.: Tyndale House, 1998), p. 155.

4. R. Kent Hughes, *1,00l Great Stories & Quotes* (Wheaton, Ill.: Tyndale House, 1998), p. 135.

5. Gary Dausey, *Practical Christianity* (Wheaton, Ill.: Tyndale House, 1987), p. 178.

6. Bruce B. Barton, et al., *Life Application Bible Commentary, John* (Wheaton, Ill.: Tyndale House, 1993), p. 123.

7. John Piper, *Desiring God* (Portland: Multnomah, 1986), pp. 197-198.

8. F. B. Meyer, *F. B. Meyer Bible Commentary* (Wheaton, Ill.: Tyndale House, 1984), p. 587.

9. Joanne Shetler, *And the Word Came with Power* (Portland: Multnomah, 1992), p. 17.

10. Kenneth N. Taylor, *The Book for Children* (Wheaton, Ill.: Tyndale House, 1985), p. 108.

11. Warren W. Wiersbe, *The Bible Exposition Commentary*, Volume I (Wheaton, Ill.: Victor Books, 1989), p. 300.

12. James S. Hewett, *Illustrations Unlimited* (Wheaton, Ill.: Tyndale House, 1988), p. 264.

13. "As with Gladness Men of Old," *The Worshiping Church* (Carol Stream, Ill.: Hope Publishing Company, 1990), p. 181.

[14]F. B. Meyer, *F. B. Meyer Bible Commentary* (Wheaton, Ill.: Tyndale House, 1984), p. 181.

[15]"When All Thy Mercies," *The Worship and Service Hymnal* (Chicago: Hope Publishing Company, 1968), p. 9.

[16]Michael Horton, *We Believe* (Nashville: Word, 1998), pp. 26-27.

[17]Michael Horton, *We Believe* (Nashville: Word, 1998), p. 51.

[18]Ronald F. Youngblood, ed., *Nelson's New Illustrated Bible Dictionary* (Nashville: Thomas Nelson, 1986), p. 503.

[19]R. Kent Hughes, *The Gift* (Wheaton, Ill.: Crossway Books, 1994), pp. 38-39.

[20]Helen Russ Stough, *A Mother's Year* (Old Tappan, N.J.: Fleming H. Revell, 1905), p. 154.

[21]Pat Alexander, *The Lion Encyclopedia of the Bible* (Oxford, England: Lion Publishing, 1986), p. 144.

[22]Michael Horton, *We Believe* (Nashville: Word , 1998), p. 101.

[23]"Hallelujah, What a Savior," *The Worshiping Church Hymnal* (Carol Stream, Ill.: Hope Publishing Company, 1990), p. 226.

[24]Michael Horton, *We Believe* (Nashville: Word, 1998), p. 131.

[25]Michael Horton, *We Believe* (Nashville: Word, 1998), p. 147.

[26]Bruce B. Barton, et al., *Life Application Bible Commentary, John* (Wheaton, Ill.: Tyndale House, 1993), pp. 300-301.

[27]Ronald F. Youngblood, ed., *Nelson's New Illustrated Bible Dictionary* (Nashville: Thomas Nelson, 1995), p. 573.

[28]Michael Horton, *We Believe* (Nashville: Word, 1998), p. 184.

[29]Michael Horton, *We Believe* (Nashville: Word, 1998), pp. 195-196.

[30]Michael Horton, *We Believe* (Nashville: Word, 1998), p. 225.

[31]Warren W. Wiersbe, *Wiersbe's Expository Outlines* (Wheaton, Ill.: Scripture Press, 1992), p. 158.

[32]Martin Marty, "Elements of Worship," in *Practical Christianity* (Wheaton, Ill.: Tyndale House, 1987), p. 358.

[33]*Chicago Tribune*, December 26, 1998 (Arts Section, page 1).

[34]Ronald F. Youngblood, ed., *Nelson's New Illustrated Bible Dictionary* (Nashville: Thomas Nelson, 1995), p. 1087.

[35]Ibid., p. 445.

_____

_____

_____

_____

_____

_____

_____

_____

_____

_____

_____

_____

_____

_____